990 by Allyn and Bacon

Simon & Schuster, Inc.
eet
ghts, Massachusetts 02194

519-0

ngress Cataloging-in-Publication Data not
ress time.

United States of America

4 3 2 1   95 94 93 92 91 90

Book Club offers books and cassettes.
write: 230 Livingston Street, Northvale,
47.

Danie

Fore

Bosto

Contents

Family therapy began in the 1950s when therapists in various parts of the United States began to study the interaction of family members. Instead of focusing on the individual as the "problem," they shifted the focus to the family unit as the problem. This shift was not simply another way of looking at the family, but represented a new model or paradigm through which the family is viewed. These early pioneers were creating new ways of seeing family process and were not simply searching for techniques.

Among these leaders was Murray Bowen, one of the first psychiatrists to put whole families in the hospital in order to observe their interaction. From these observations, Bowen began to hypothesize that schizophrenia is a three-generational, evolutionary process. This close contact with families allowed him to postulate the concept of differentiation of self, which became one of the building blocks of his theory. Michael Kerr, in his foreword that follows, gives a more detailed description of this process.

Most of the early pioneers in the field have moved into other areas of research, but Dr. Bowen has continued to develop and refine his theory. One cannot begin to study the field of family therapy without studying Murray Bowen. He is to the field what Immanuel Kant is to the history of modern philosophy: the one person who is the starting point on the journey of knowledge. Many of his ideas (e.g., differentiation, family projection process, and triangles) have become part of all family therapy theory, regardless of one's school of thought. In brief, Bowen family therapy has become the *lingua franca* of the field.

In March 1970 the Group for Advancement of Psychiatry published a study of family therapy based on a questionnaire issued in 1967. The therapists involved in the study were asked to name those theorists they regarded as most important to their field. Those named included Virginia Satir, Nathan Ackerman, Don Jackson, Jay Haley, and Murray Bowen. Still active in the field, Haley has spent most of his time developing "techniques" of working with family problems and little time on theory. Dr. Bowen, on the other hand, has chosen to study how the family unit is governed. It is his belief that therapy is a result of how one conceptualizes the family process and views its interaction, and that therapy cannot be divorced from family theory.

What is the Bowen theory of family process? Dr. Papero's text is an in-depth explanation of it. It is the first full-length study of Bowen theory written by one who is associated with Dr. Bowen and has been a part of the ongoing process of his thought. It is the product of Bowen theory from the "inside."

Clearly Murray Bowen's theory ranked as a high priority. Finding someone who understands its intricacies and can present it clearly with all its richness was a major task. After much consultation, Dr. Papero was asked to undertake the project. We now have the results, and for the first time a reader in the field of family therapy has a text that explains both the theory and the therapy of Murray Bowen.

Vincent D. Foley
Jamaica Estates, New York

Foreword

It is difficult to say when anyone "begins" a career of discovery. The capacity to look at the same things others have looked at and to see things no one has seen before is probably part of an orientation to the world that is evident in childhood. Murray Bowen's "formal" career of discovery in psychiatry began in 1946 at the Menninger Clinic in Topeka, Kansas. Bowen had served as a general medical officer in the Army from 1941–1945, and his wartime experiences significantly influenced his decision to specialize in psychiatry. Psychiatric casualties were very common during the war, and many young physicians became interested in developing more understanding of such problems. The Menninger Clinic was a premier institution for training in this exciting and rapidly growing specialty.

Bowen was not in psychiatry very long before he began to question the soundness of the field's basic theoretical foundations, foundations that rested in the formulations of Sigmund Freud. The Menninger Clinic had a strong psychoanalytic orientation, and Bowen was being trained accordingly. He was an avid student. Yet while considering many of Freud's contributions to be enormously important and valuable, Bowen gradually came to believe that many of Freud's most influential theoretical ideas were subjective and that the amount of subjectivity effectively precluded Freudian theory from ever becoming an accepted science. Freud had striven toward a scientific base for his formulations about human behavior, but too many of his central concepts had no basis in the life sciences. For example, the Oedipus complex came from literature, not from science. Bowen has argued that Freud was aware of the uncertain base of many of his theoretical ideas, but that many students of Freud treated those ideas as if they were facts.

Perhaps like Freud, Bowen came to believe early in his career that human behavior could become an accepted science. This belief has shaped his professional life course for more than forty years. For the study of human behavior to become an accepted science, the concepts developed about it would have to be consistent with knowledge that had and would emerge in all branches of the life sciences. So one of

Bowen's first steps toward exploring the possibilities for a scientific theory of human behavior was to read extensively in the sciences, particularly in biology and evolutionary theory. What human beings *imagine* the world to be is one thing; what the world *is* is something else. Imagination is part of human subjectivity. Verifiable facts about the planets, the earth, and all living things are part of science. Man's effort to make his thinking more consistent with the factual world is part of human objectivity. Bowen attempted to make his thinking about human emotional functioning and behavior as consistent as possible with this factual world. An important effort was that concepts about human behavior should be grounded in the ways that human beings are *similar* to all life rather than the ways that human beings are a *unique* species.

Bowen's reading in the natural sciences coupled with his extensive research and clinical experience with families of patients who had a wide range of psychiatric and other diagnoses led to his developing a new theory of human emotional functioning and behavior, *family systems theory*. The theory conceptualizes the family as a naturally occurring system that exhibits patterns of emotional functioning that are related to patterns observed in subhuman species. The clinical dysfunctions (physical, emotional, and social) are linked to these emotionally governed patterns that man has in common with the lower forms. Furthermore, Bowen theorized that differences in the emotional functioning of families are quantitative rather than qualitative in nature.

The conceptualization of the family as an emotionally governed system or unit (emotion is synonymous with instinct, not feeling) was a radical departure from accepted psychiatric theory of the time and led almost automatically to an equally radical new form of therapy, therapy directed at the family unit. If this conceptualization is accurate, then therapy directed at *any* family member, not just the symptomatic member, can modify the whole unit. Changes in the functioning of *one* family member are followed predictably by changes in the functioning of other family members, even the symptomatic ones. It is not necessary to have the symptomatic family member in therapy for the symptoms to be relieved. Family therapy does not mean treatment for the whole family. It is therapy based on a way of thinking that conceptualizes a reciprocity in functioning between family members.

Bowen left the Menninger Clinic in 1954 and organized a family research project at the National Institute of Mental Health in Rockville, Maryland. The project, which lasted until 1959, involved having entire nuclear families live on a research ward for an extended period. Many of the somewhat loosely knit ideas that Bowen had developed while at Menninger merged into coherent concepts during the NIMH period.

These concepts, along with others that were developed later, became the basis for family systems theory. In 1959, Bowen moved to the Department of Psychiatry, Georgetown University Medical Center, Washington, D.C., where he has remained until the present time. Some important developments in theory and therapy have occurred during his tenure at Georgetown. One of these makes this book by Dr. Daniel Papero especially important. To place this development in context, however, it is necessary to go back to the beginning of the family movement.

The family movement surfaced in the mental health world at the American Orthopsychiatric and American Psychiatric Association meetings in the spring of 1957. Prior to 1957, a number of investigators were studying the family, but with little knowledge of one another's work. The shared vision of those pioneering family researchers was that the study of the family had the potential to alter drastically our understanding of the forces that govern individual development and behavior. Several of these researchers envisioned that individual theory would eventually be replaced by a theory based on an understanding of the family as a unit. However, family therapy, not family theory, captured the interest and enthusiasm of the mental health world. The potential of the family movement for radically altering man's view of himself, and for moving toward a science of human behavior, was lost. By the mid 1970s, the emphasis on therapeutic techniques had resulted in the development of numerous "schools" of family therapy. Distinctions between major leaders in the family field were made largely on the basis of how they were perceived to conduct therapy. Important theoretical distinctions in the field were largely obscured.

An important development occurred at Georgetown during the late 1960s that markedly accentuated the perception that Bowen, like other major leaders in the field, was best distinguished by his particular approach to therapy, not by his theoretical formulations. The development was the expansion of the therapeutic focus from the nuclear to the extended family. Based on a solid theoretical understanding of the extended family system (the concept of triangles was a particularly important component of this understanding), Bowen defined ways in which people could change *while in active relationship to* their parents, siblings, and other emotionally significant people in their family of origin. It is not necessary to cut off from the family to manage the problems generated by being involved with it. There is an alternative that is based on seeing oneself as part of the system and working to change oneself in relationship to it. A focus on the extended family has some distinct advantages over an exclusive focus on the nuclear family.

Once this new therapeutic approach had been presented nationally by Bowen and then others who worked with him, mental-health professionals literally flocked to Georgetown to learn how to deal with their families of origin. It was an important, exciting, and radical development in psychotherapy. As was the case in 1957, in the minds of many people the importance of sound theoretical understanding to the success of a therapeutic effort was lost. Many people did and still do attempt to pry themselves loose from their unresolved attachments to their families by using a base in individual theory. Because individual theory does not conceptualize the complex family relationship system, it is not an adequate theoretical base for guiding an effort in the family of origin. Without an understanding of the relationship system as a whole, people are highly vulnerable to falling into the same old emotional patterns, Failing to get a balanced view, they blame the family too much or they blame themselves too much.

Other groups around the country soon became interested in some version of therapy that focused on the extended or multigenerational family. Most of the approaches developed by these groups bore little resemblance to what has been developed at Georgetown. Despite marked divergences in theoretical viewpoints, however, Bowen and the Georgetown family program were usually grouped in meetings, journals, and books with others who did "extended (or multigenerations) family therapy." This grouping occurred although some therapists who focused on the family of origin did it from a clearly espoused base in psychoanalytic theory, while Georgetown focused on the family of origin from a base that viewed the family as a naturally occurring, emotionally governed system. These groupings based on therapy rather than on theory reflect a trend in the family movement that began in 1957.

This volume by Dr. Daniel Papero is important because it emphasizes family as a new theory as well as a new method of therapy. The principles that guide family psychotherapy are a logical outgrowth of theory. The volume is unique by virtue of its presentation of a broad perspective on human emotional functioning and behavior in a concise way. If people are presented with too many details, their ability to see the "whole" may be undermined. If people are presented with too few details, they may find it difficult to see theory other than as a difficult-to-apply abstraction. Dr. Papero has split the difference between "too much" and "too little" rather nicely. Dr. Papero was a logical choice to write a book about Bowen Theory for two reasons: (1) his knowledge of theory and therapy and (2) his ongoing effort to define as clearly as he can where Bowen ends and Papero begins.

Michael Kerr, M.D.
Washington, DC

Daniel Papero, Ph.D., has been important in the long-term development of Bowen Family Systems Theory. His professional life has been dedicated to theory. It began when he heard about the theory while he worked at the Veterans Administration Hospital attached to Vanderbilt Medical Center in Nashville. It grew through the 1970s when he was in the Special Postgraduate training program at the Family Center. That program was in Washington, three full days, four times a year. He was on a responsible life course to learn more and more. During that period, he used every opportunity to supplement training and to move toward presenting professional papers at the Annual Georgetown Family Symposium. That had long been a forum for the best in theoretical and clinical presentation.

His untiring quest for knowledge led to the most important decision in his life. In the early 1980s, he gave up his salaried position in Nashville and moved his young family to Washington, where his income would be determined by a part-time private practice. It was a major move for him and for the Family Center. Faculty members usually made a living from part-time practices in the community, while they donated half their professional time to the Family Center for the privilege of being associated with a successful organization. Dr. Papero is a gifted individual. The Family Center went an extra mile to help him get started. He was close within the Family Center. He agreed to assume increasing responsibility and to work without a salary with low fee "clinic" patients. The Family Center agreed to provide him with an office and to help him with a part-time private practice. In due time, he was able to increase the part-time private practice income to a livable level for his family.

The arrangement with Dr. Papero, when the Family Center had limited office space, has proved to be one of the most fortunate decisions ever made, both for him and the Family Center. The result appears to be a combination of theory and individuality to make it consistent with the way I have lived my own life. When a problem has existed within the Family Center staff, theory would say I played a part in it. If I can discover and correct the part I play, all the others will automatically correct their parts. An administration based on systems theory is different from one in which each boss tells others what to do. It creates a situation in which the emphasis is on individual responsibility. Each is striving to become the best they can become. It is a happy environment. If one falters, there is another to take his or her place, without being critical of the "differentiation of self," an important concept in theory. Dr. Papero is a responsible person. When that level of responsibility is put into an environment that encourages responsibility, it is a healthy combination. He is in the Family Center all day, every day. He is in a position of saying, "The Family Center is mine to run to the best of my ability." As time passed, and he assumed more responsibility for knowing and extending theory and integrating it with training courses, seminars, symposia, family therapy, and everyday running of the Center, he became essential in teaching an accurate version of the theory to those who come to learn. There is no question about Dr. Papero being an absolute master of the many factual variables of the theory, as they exist at the present time.

There are questions about the future of theory, as it proceeds through the centuries. When I created Family Systems Theory in the 1950s, there was a disciplined effort to create a method of thinking based on facts alone. There are problems in such an effort. Any theory about the human is filled with certain immutable facts. It also contacts the effervescent feelings of those who apply the theory. As the theory passes from one person to another, it is unwittingly tinged with feelings, which dilute the theory in a process called "erosion." At the Family Center, a continuing effort has resisted the erosion, in the belief that mental health will finally benefit when theorists of the future can separate facts from feelings. The human is a feeling being, but the effervescent personal feelings can be handled as a function of the human without diluting the impersonal theory. Numerous diluted versions of Family Systems Theory have emerged, as the theory passes from one person to another, but the dilution has been far less than would be anticipated in usual circumstances. The profession is proceeding steadily toward a theory based on immutable facts. The trend of events may be related to the discipline that went into the creation of a theory based on facts.

This foreword is directed to Dr. Papero and his dedication to theory. He is one and I am another. He surely has some individual perceptions that are different from mine, but he has worked closely with me for many years, and his presentation of Bowen Family Systems Theory is one of the best.

Murray Bowen, M.D.
Washington, DC

Murray Bowen's influence on the study of the human family is immeasurable. Hardly a paper or article is presented today without some reference to his work. Any original thinker and researcher attracts followers. That is both a help and a hindrance. In fortunate circumstances the learner can carry a trailblazer's work forward into new areas of exploration. When followers become proselytizers of a new "truth," the outcome is far different.

The opportunity to write about the ideas of a pioneer in the area of family study does not come often, at least in the format of this series. I have experienced it as a thrill and a challenge. The act of writing combines the effects of an Xray and a Rorschach administered to the self. In fine, sometimes painful, detail one sees the truncated skeleton of one's knowledge and the fantasies of understanding the pacesetting work of another. Every concept, and in fact every sentence, must be as accurate as possible, yet complete accuracy is ever elusive. The written paragraph never quite captures the point to be made. In the end I have come to realize what should have been obvious at the onset. The following volume represents more of my thinking about the human family than it captures that of Dr. Bowen. Caveat lector!

My special thanks go to Dr. Murray Bowen, whose work and endless questions have stimulated my thinking and productivity far beyond my expectations. Dr. Michael Kerr has offered insight and encouragement, originally as a teacher and more recently as a colleague. I come increasingly to appreciate the depth of his understanding and the solidness of his thinking. The faculty members and clinical associates of the Family Center have been a steady resource, although they are probably not individually aware of the degree to which each contributed to my learning. The administrative staff of the Family Center — Ruth Sagar, Marjorie Hottel, Mary Ann Lancaster, Kathy Vlahos, and Rebecca Rose — have been generous with their time and helpful with their comments and suggestions. And finally series editor Vincent Foley has displayed the patience of Job and made thoughtful suggestions that have improved the overall quality of the work.

My own clinical experience with families began in 1974 when I was associated with the Dede Wallac Community Mental Health Center in Nashville, Tennessee. Two colle gues in those years, Ruth Patton and Shirley Wrightsman, recognized my interest in the family. Neither they nor I would have foreseen this volume, but their influence and insight remains with me today. I was a fortunate novice, indeed. A special note of thanks must be reserved for the families I have seen professionally over the years. In each instance they have granted me the privilege of learning about them, tolerated my sometimes primitive questions, and taught me important lessons of respect for the complexities and the dignity of the human family.

Finally a special kind of appreciation is reserved for the family into which I was born and the family I helped to create through marriage. While they would not agree with all my points of view nor even with my understanding of family, I believe they have appreciated and supported my efforts to understand. My children, Laura and Anna, have endured me with humor. I am particularly grateful to my spouse, Patricia Howell Papero. Her broad perspective and innate good sense have made her a valued critic. She has led me to reflect upon the arrogance of my postures as expert and helped me gradually to understand better the parameters of my own vast subjectivity.

Washington, DC

Chapter 1

Bowen Theory in Perspective

Human behavior, viewed from a broad perspective, has been remarkably constant since *Homo sapiens* first appeared on the planet. Man reproduces, raises offspring, attends to needs for shelter and sustenance, and seeks to establish and defend a home range or territory as have his ancestors across the millennia. Like all other life-forms, man is a product of the earth and is intimately connected to it.

How the human has approached and managed the dual biological mandates of self-preservation and reproduction is seemingly unique in the history of life on Earth. Equipped with his marvelous brain, man has a range of flexibility apparently unmatched by his animate cousins. That brain and its variety of responses have made it extremely difficult for humankind to study itself. The incredible manifestations of human behavior contain thousands of alluring byways and dead ends that captivate attention and absorb research energy. One can become fascinated with the display and miss the underlying function of behavior in the process of life.

Yet people have also been aware of or at least believed in an orderliness to life even in the face of chaos. At some point the early human intelligence became capable of observing the tides, the patterns of the stars, and the cycle of the seasons. Life forms have long responded to such phenomena. But to observe and reflect upon them added a new dimension. It had within it the seeds of science, religion, philosophy, and mathematics.

The ability to observe produced mysteries and questions. Stories, images, and myths were used to fill in the gaps and to explain phenomena. Some also studied the gaps and mysteries, further developing the ability to observe. It became possible at times to use facts to explain phenomena without recourse to imagination. Science was born when it became possible to distinguish the quest for intuitive truth from the search for factual knowledge.

For man to observe and study himself has been the most difficult task of all. It is relatively easy to be objective about those aspects of nature and the universe that appear to be least involved in human life. Medieval scientists looked to the heavens and pondered stellar mysteries. Even today it is easier for man to explain the birth of the stars than to understand the nature of human aggression. Subjectivity colors, clouds, and distorts man's ability to view himself. It is extremely difficult for the human to think about or observe human behavior without automatically responding. A good example involves the idea of love. It is an arduous if not impossible task to find agreement on a definition of love. What can be generally agreed upon is that use of the term *love* produces a personal, often feeling-laden point of view in humans. This automatic, generally affective response is the essence of subjectivity.

Darwin's ideas on the development of life through evolution moved humanity a giant step closer to an objective view of itself. Human development was linked to that of all life. *Homo sapiens* was a product of evolution and responsive to the pressures of evolutionary development. Although as a species humankind can be somewhat more objective about its origins and less sure of its unique position on the planet, it remains difficult for the individual to move beyond a personalized, that is, subjective, view of him- or herself.

The subjective nature of the study of human behavior has created obstacles to its acceptance among the natural sciences. Nonetheless there have been those who sustain the belief that a scientific study of human behavior is possible. Bowen Family Systems Theory is the product of one effort toward that end.

Modern psychiatric thinking rests essentially on psychoanalytic theory, which sees the human as unique and different from other life-forms. In spite of its unquestioned contributions, psychoanalytic theory has not attained general scientific acceptance. Bowen wondered why psychiatry was not a science (Bowen, 1982a).* In his quest for a theory, he read extensively from numerous disciplines, looking for the ideas on which the disciplines were based. Out of this process came "the notion of the human as a phylogenetic development from lower forms of life" (Bowen, 1982b, p. 1). Bowen Theory is the product of an effort

---

*Much of the information about the development of Dr. Bowen's thinking comes from my recollection of personal conversations, presentations which I heard, and my general exposure to papers and talks that never formally reached publication. Some have been published in newsletters and other organs with limited circulation. Where possible, I will give these references. Where this is not possible, the reader is cautioned to remember the subjective nature of human recall and regard the written word with appropriate suspicion.

to develop a scientific approach to the study of human behavior focusing on man's relatedness to all life.

Family theory and therapy play a small role in the professional activities of the mental-health field. Generally they are considered an offshoot of the psychological disciplines with little direct usefulness or insight to offer outside the limited realm of psychotherapeutic treatment. Among family clinicians, family therapy is seen generally as a relatively new and promising series of techniques to alter and ameliorate human distress. The focus remains on the symptomatic individual, and family therapy is viewed as an important tool in an armamentarium for relief of distress.

A much smaller number of individuals work to develop and expand the theoretical base for understanding the human family. For them family theory promises a new way of looking at the world, a fresher and fuller understanding of the nature and mechanics of human behavior than has previously been possible. In this framework, theoretical understanding leads to technique. The goal, therefore, becomes expanded understanding of human family behavior.

That members of a family influence one another is a long-standing part of folk wisdom. People have long remarked "like father, like son" and known about Cain and Abel. Careful observers have noted characteristics of such influences that repeat themselves within a family cluster of individuals. This web of interconnection and influence has come generally and at times imprecisely to be called the *family system*. Under this general label the focus of study may be the two-person relationship or dyad, the family unit of parents and children (in its many variations) or nuclear family, or the relationships among or between members of several generations, the extended family.

A major theoretical framework guiding the study of the human family system bears the rather plain title General System Theory.* Introduced by the biologist and mathematician Ludwig von Bertalanffy before the Second World War, General System Theory is a collection of ideas drawn from specific theories in various branches of science. It attempts to define principles found universally in all systems in nature. In its purest or classical sense, General System Theory uses mathematics to define principles that apply to systems in general (Bertalanffy, 1968, p. 16). The term *system* in this context refers to the operation of organisms or wholes, seen as entities and not as constellations of parts.

---

*In current usage one commonly sees the term *General Systems Theory*. The usage here corresponds to Bertalanffy's usage of the term and omits the s from the word *system*.

As a framework or template for guiding thought and research, General System Theory has been applied in many areas to give new insight to old observations and to open new frontiers of thought. A fine and relatively early example of such application can be noted in the work of Talcott Parsons on organizational behavior. Concepts like *homeostasis, entropy,* and *open* and *closed system* reflect the presence of General System Theory in the family field. What basically is being said is that the family acts as if the principles of General System Theory were shaping the course and its development.

Bowen also used the word *system* to describe what he saw. In a 1966 paper, he explained that the family was a system because a change in one part produces compensatory change in other parts of the family (Bowen, 1966). In this sense the operation of family systems would be similar to that of known natural systems, for example the human cardiovascular system. In 1975, Bowen added his own name to the original title Family Systems Theory to avoid an increasing imprecision in the general usage of the word *system.* (In this volume, the term Bowen Theory will be used interchangeably with Bowen Family Systems Theory.)

Bowen Theory and General System Theory have areas in common yet spring from quite different roots. As noted previously, General System Theory is derived from mathematics and human thought. Bowen Theory rests on factual knowledge gained from direct observation of the human family. Like Goodall with the chimpanzee, Schaller with the Serengeti lion and other species, or Fossey with the mountain gorilla, Bowen has conducted a long-term field study of human behavior.

By broadening perspective, Bowen worked to see the orderly processes that govern human emotional behavior. Working always with a view toward the day when a science of the human could join with and be accepted by the other natural sciences, he paid particular attention to the use of terms to describe and communicate his work. The language of Bowen Theory is generally taken from biology and used in an identical or closely related sense to its usage there. A basic assumption that human emotional illness is rooted in biology guided the research.

The perceptive reader will have already noted the use of the term *emotional illness* in place of the more conventional *mental illness.* The change of terminology highlights an important notion in Bowen Theory. Emotion in this sense refers to the automatic processes governing life on all levels, from the cellular to the societal. Bowen describes what is meant as follows.

> It [emotional functioning] includes the force that biology defines as
> instinct, reproduction, the automatic activity controlled by the
> autonomic nervous system, subjective emotional and feeling states,
> and the forces that govern relationship systems In broad terms, the
> emotional system governs the 'dance of life' in all living things
> (Bowen, 1975, p. 380).

Such an automatic guidance system is believed to operate according to principles that are knowable and that can be used to predict
behavior. Bowen Theory represents an effort to define in an initial
fashion the operating principles for the human. By definition the human
emotional system is assumed to be a version of that which governs the
behavior of all animate life.

If the human emotional system is akin to the guidance systems of
other living things, then information acquired in animal studies may be
of illustrative importance. In broadening the focus of thinking beyond
the human to nature and other life-forms, one has to be clear about the
role of analogy in such thought.

There are characteristics of an amoeba or a troop of gorillas which,
from a certain perspective, appear similar to characteristics of the human.
But such a comparison does not imply that the processes are factually
the same. Since a theory can only be developed on the foundation of
fact, the use of analogy can do no more than contribute to the expansion
of perspective and thought. Yet it is not always clear where analogy
stops and factual congruence occurs. Such points of congruence, if
significant enough, can contribute to the development of a broader
theory or set of principles than those that guided the initial research.

Through analogy, the work of two scientists at the National
Institute of Mental Health (NIMH) has been helpful in understanding
the notion of the emotional system.* Paul D. MacLean, Chief of the
Laboratory of Brain Evolution and Behavior, has studied brain structures
and their functions which relate to emotional behavior in laboratory
animals, generally cats and monkeys. John B. Calhoun, of the section on
behavioral systems of the same laboratory, has tried "to discover what
external conditions enhanced or inhibited the developmental welfare of
individuals and populations" (Calhoun, 1974, p. 16).

MacLean's work has greatly expanded the understanding of the
physiological structures and pathways of emotional behavior in mammals. His concept of the triune brain is best stated in his own words:

---

*The discussion here of the work of Drs. Calhoun and MacLean is in no way an
exhaustive presentation of their many contributions. The curious reader is directed to
the scientific literature where each fully represents his own thought.

In its evolution the human forebrain has expanded to great size while retaining the basic features of three formations that reflect our ancestral relationship to reptiles, early mammals and recent mammals. Radically different in structure and chemistry, and in an evolutionary sense countless generations apart, the three formations constitute a hierarchy of three brains in one, or what may be called in short a triune brain (MacLean, 1978, pp. 308-309).

MacLean is not attempting to say that the human has in fact three brains. Each of the structures, however, relates to the internal and external worlds of the organism quite differently. Furthermore, the two older structures, the R-complex and the limbic system, do not possess the neural mechanisms for verbal communication.

Much of MacLean's research has focused on the function of the two evolutionarily older brain structures, the R-complex and the limbic system. Deep in the center of the brain, the R-complex is comprised of the olfactostriatum, the corpus striatum, the globus pallidus, and satellite collections of gray matter (MacLean, 1978). Structurally and chemically it is similar to the brain of a reptile. The limbic system comprises the limbic cortex and the structures of the brainstem with which it has primary connections (MacLean, 1970). Included in the limbic system are the cingulate gyrus, the hippocampus, the hippocampal gyrus, the amygdala, and the septum.

The R-complex appears to play a major role in the various behavioral displays used in social communication and in the behaviors which form the basis of conspecific recognition. MacLean coined the term *prosematic* to refer to any sort of nonverbal signal — vocal, chemical, or behavioral. While such signals may be intentional (active) or unintentional (passive), they have meaning and an orderly arrangement (MacLean, 1982a). The performance of like kinds of behavior forms the basis of species identification. (MacLean uses the term *isopraxis* to denote the performance of like kinds of behavior.)

A series of elegant experiments form the basis for such conclusions. The squirrel monkey (*Saimiri sciureus*) performs a particular display in shows of aggression and courtship. In such situations, the male makes a vocal sound, spreads his thighs, and directs his erect phallus toward the other animal. One variety of squirrel monkey (identified as the "gothic" because of a colored patch above the eye resembling a gothic arch) accomodatingly will perform this display upon seeing its own reflection in a mirror. MacLean and his assistants observed the effect of carefully located brain lesions on this automatic, innate display. Lesions in the pallidal structures produced lasting effects on the observed display. In contrast, damage to other parts of the brain, including the destruction of large parts of the limbic system, had little or no lasting effect on the display (MacLean, 1978).

A later series focused on the male green anolis lizard (*Anolis carolinensis*). In this animal there is an almost complete optic decussation (the optic nerves from each eye cross almost completely to the opposite hemisphere). This anatomical configuration allowed the researchers to perform lesions in only one hemisphere, providing certain experimental advantages. Once again a particular display was observed before and after damage to the brain. Once again the results implicated the striatal areas in the organized expression of species-typical displays (Greenberg, MacLean, & Ferguson, 1979).

More than twenty patterns of behavior are held in common by reptiles and mammals. These behaviors involve self-preservation and the survival of the species. MacLean defines five general categories of behavior that may be operative in the patterns mentioned above. This "pentad" of interoperative behaviors are denoted as (1) isopraxic, in which two or more individuals engage in the same kind of activity; (2) perseverative, in which an individual repeats certain behaviors like the display; (3) reenactive, in which an individual appears to repeat certain acts as if following a precedent; (4) tropistic, characterized by positive or negative responses to partial or complete representations of another; and (5) deceptive, involving the use of artifice and deceit (MacLean, 1972). The pentad is observable in reptiles and mammals, including the human. MacLean's research implicates the R-complex in all such behaviors.

The structurally primitive limbic cortex is essentially similar in all mammals (MacLean, 1958). Receiving information from both internally and externally oriented sensory systems, the limbic system is concerned with emotional functions relating to self-preservation and reproduction. The product of the integration of internal and external sensory information in the limbic system can only be subjectively experienced as feeling or affect. The behavioral product of an affective state, which is observable, can be defined as emotion (MacLean, 1970). MacLean defines three types of affect. Basic affects are information of bodily needs recognized as hunger, thirst, and the various feeling manifestations of bodily processes. Specific affects occur with the activation of a particular sensory system as when feeling pain after a noxious stimulus. General affects are feelings which pertain to situations, individuals, and groups and concern self-preservation and preservation of the species.

Although the limbic system receives both internal and external sensory input, MacLean's research suggests that internal signals have the overriding influence on neuronal discharge. In other words, the limbic-based behavior of an individual occurs to the beat of an internal drummer.

Feeling and the sense of conviction can be completely internal and have no relationship to, or even contradict, external reality. Under the guidance of the limbic system the individual may react to external stimuli on the basis of an internally guided perception of reality (MacLean, 1970).

The evolution from reptiles to mammals is marked by three behavioral advances: (1) nursing, (2) parental care, and (3) a warm-blooded condition (MacLean, 1982a). In a series of experiments with Syrian golden hamsters (*Mesocricetus auratus*), MacLean and his colleagues demonstrated the role of the limbic system in these behaviors and in a fourth mammalian development, play (Murphy, MacLean, & Hamilton, 1981). Within the first 48 hours after the animal's birth, the neocortex was removed. Those animals without the neocortex were then simply observed as they grew. The experimental animals grew at a normal rate and with the typical developmental timing of the species. In subsequent trials, the neocortex and the midline limbic structures (the cingulate convolution and the underlying dorsal sections of the hippocampus) were destroyed. These animals retained many species-typical behaviors but displayed no play during development and showed major deficits in maternal behavior. The research demonstrated that "in a rodent ...the striatal complex and limbic system, with the remaining neuraxis, are sufficient for giving expression to a wide range of unlearned forms of species-typical behavior and that the midline limbic structures are required for the expression of play behavior and integrated performance of maternal behavior" (Murphy et al., 1981, p. 461).

The limbic cortex can be divided into three main divisions. Two of the three are associated with the olfactory apparatus and are involved in self-preservation and self-protection. The third section, within the upper part of the limbic convolution, MacLean refers to as the *great arc* (MacLean, 1982b). Not only is the great arc implicated in play and maternal behavior, but additional research indicates that the rostral end of the arc is required for the spontaneous production of the isolation call, the most fundamental and elemental of all mammalian vocalizations. This evidence, along with the connections between the great arc and the frontal lobes, lead MacLean to the following observation: "Indeed, one might say that the history of the evolution of mammals is to a large extent the history of the evolution of the family" (MacLean, 1982b, p. 304).

MacLean's work on the function of the R-complex and limbic system in emotional expression and behavior points toward the definition of an emotional system that is similar in a general way to that proposed by Bowen. It suggests the neural machinery that might underlie such an emotional component within an individual. It suggests, further, that much of human behavior may be automatic and outside of human awareness, let alone control. More importantly, it fits the development of the human family into evolution and places the human brain alongside all of its evolutionary forebears. Such a view of the human family is rooted in biology and points in the same direction as Bowen Theory, which assumes the basic commonality of all living things.

John B. Calhoun's journey from a Tennessee childhood to the position of major researcher is a fascinating story (Calhoun, 1977). He reports, in retrospect, that three related ideas guided his research: (1) population, (2) environmental design, and (3) social consciousness, mental health, and human evolution. Those ideas led him initially to academia and eventually to the National Institute of Mental Health (NIMH), where for several years he pursued these themes in major experiments involving population density and environmental designs.

Working generally with populations of laboratory mice and rats, Calhoun studied the effects of population density on animals within a specially constructed habitat or "universe." There are many points of interest to the family theorist in Calhoun's work. In general they concern the effect of other animals upon an individual in a stable environment. In his experimental habitats or universes, Calhoun essentially allowed populations to grow without the usual environmental restraints. The result was increasing population density within the universes. As density increased, so did general pathology, or the inability to adjust to changing conditions (Calhoun, 1971).

Calhoun's first major universe followed from his work as a researcher at Johns Hopkins University studying the urban rat in the city of Baltimore. Because of the difficulties studying the animals in their urban settings, Calhoun decided to construct a habitat that closely resembled the Baltimore row house environment. The outcome was a large pen (100 feet in diameter) constructed in an open space adjacent to Calhoun's rental house.

The colony was begun with the introduction of five pairs of wild rats assumed to be as genetically similar as possible for animals trapped in the wild state. The rats were trapped on an island in the Chesapeake Bay that had been cut off from the mainland about 45 years previously. It could reasonably be presumed that genetic drift would have led to a significant degree of homozygosity. The research outcomes, therefore, could be judged the product of environmental factors and not hereditary differences among the animals (Calhoun, 1963). Several general observations from the field studies in the Baltimore row house neighborhoods led to the research hypothesis. "The growth rate of a population will be inhibited in the absence of predation and in the presence of an excess of food and harborage. This inhibition arises through the social interaction among the members of the population with respect to the distribution of goals and barriers through the environment" (Calhoun, 1963, p. 2).

Calhoun's "backyard" project continued for 27 months. The rat population increased as predicted and then leveled off. Early in the history of the project the more dominant animals tended to occupy a particular area within the pen (the southeastern half). This territorial structure was maintained for the entire study (Calhoun, 1963). As the population grew, competition between animals increased, driving some rats from the early and higher ranking colonies in the southeastern portion of the pen. The migrating animals were primarily male and of lower social status. Such migration led to increasing social interaction among animals of the newer, socially lower ranking colonies.

With time there came to be an excess of males in the northwestern sector of the pen (Calhoun, 1963). Within this area no male was able to clearly establish a territory. Females within this area, when in estrus, tended to be pursued by packs of males. Often a female would be mounted frequently (Calhoun estimates as much as a thousand times in one night), and her behavior indicated that she was experiencing substantial stress. Such females tended to have reduced conceptions and were able to raise young only with great difficulty. Normal maternal behaviors, essential to the successful raising of the litter, were greatly inhibited or completely lacking. In contrast, in the southeastern sector of the enclosure, males were able to establish territories around several high-ranking females. Such females were not hounded by other males and were highly successful in conceiving and rearing young.

Several other interesting observations were made from the Baltimore project. While socially higher ranking rats were able to maintain a bimodal nocturnal rhythm in visiting the food pen, lower ranking individuals tended to feed only when higher ranking animals were absent. The effect was to make lower ranking individuals more active in the dawn and dusk time periods rather than the nighttime periods preferred by the more dominant rats. A second observation was that individuals born into lower ranking groups (primarily in the northwestern sector) experienced greater inhibition of growth than animals from higher ranking groups.

From this original research environment Calhoun's thinking moved to more controlled and observable settings. He moved first to Walter Reed Army Medical Center and then to the NIMH. With the move to the NIMH came access to the space needed to conduct further research. In a barn made available to the project, Calhoun constructed the research environments or "universes." Each was essentially a square enclosure of a specific size. Along the vertical walls were constructed sources for food and water as well as boxes for nesting. Ample nesting materials were available at all times. Into such prepared environments Calhoun introduced a breeding pair of mice or rats. The populations were allowed to develop essentially unchecked. As density increased, so did general pathology, defined as the inability to adjust to changing conditions (Calhoun, 1971).

The observations of such populations led to the development of several important concepts. Of particular interest is the concept of social velocity. In the laboratory, social velocity was defined as "a measure of the amount of time an individual spends in that portion of its home range or field of action where it is maximally exposed to contacting associates and then becoming involved in social interaction" (Calhoun, 1967, p. 28). Calhoun's studies indicated a predictable curve of social velocity in a group of mice. The dominant male and female had the highest rankings, and the less dominant individuals fell into place as the curve descended.

Individuals with high social velocity showed appropriate territorial behaviors. As social velocity declined, however, animals showed behaviors that appeared to deviate increasingly from those considered optimally "mouselike." On the lower end of the curve, animals tended to avoid contact with others and to be ignored by the more dominant individuals altogether. As environmental stress increased (due to population density), fewer and fewer individuals were able to maintain a high social velocity and ever greater numbers of animals exhibited behaviors common to the lowest end of the curve. Although the curve and the differences between individuals tended to be intensified under environmental stress, Calhoun concluded that even under optimal environmental conditions the social velocity curve, with attendant alterations in behavior, will develop. It is simply a predictable outcome of group living (Calhoun, 1971).

Calhoun's explanation of this apparently fixed outcome concerns the type of contact between individuals. He reasoned that contact can be gratifying, frustrating, or neutral. Each gratifying contact leads to a refractory period during which the gratified individual will not respond appropriately to meet the social need of another. The result of such a nongratifying contact is a state of frustration for the unfulfilled individual. In the natural course of group interaction, some individuals will benefit from gratifying contact much of the time and others will arrive at varying degrees of frustration. In this manner the social velocity curve develops. The inappropriate response to a needy other, whether due to gratification or frustration, Calhoun defines as aggression (Calhoun, 1971).

Calhoun goes yet a step further to suggest that through evolution a species develops a genetic constitution compatible with adjustment to the physiological consequences of frustration. This in essence implies that there is a genetically determined balance of gratification and frustration for an individual. When an individual has too many gratifying encounters, it will actively seek encounters in which the other will respond aggressively in order to maintain the physiology required by the genetic basis of the individual, that is, a balance of gratification and frustration (Calhoun, 1971).

Yet another factor in theoretical gratification – frustration basis of social velocity concerns the intensity of interaction. The length of the refractory period following contact will be proportional to the intensity of contact/interaction. "It is this accommodation of intensity of interaction to the dynamics of life in a particular sized group which leads to the origin of basic group size" (Calhoun, 1967, p. 26). The effect of increased population density is to force contact beyond that determined by optimal group size leading to alterations in the behavior of all individuals.

The intensity of contact or interaction can be influenced by the heredity and past history of the individuals involved. In a different experiment, Calhoun selected two strains of the same species, the house mouse. The strains differed from one another in the area of physiological stability (Calhoun, 1956). The research objective was to determine the extent to which heredity might modify social behavior. Introducing a pregnant female of each strain into an identical environment initiated the colonies. As population density in the colonies increased, Calhoun found deterioration of social interaction occurred rapidly among the less stable strain. These mice fought more frequently, and dispersed groups were less successful in reproducing beyond the initial litter and died off more rapidly at higher population densities. Calhoun also found that if population density increased sufficiently, even the stable strain of mice developed similar behavioral changes. The more stable strain, however, was able to function with less intense interaction in conditions that had produced extreme behavior in the less stable strain.

Calhoun, as noted previously, defined pathological behavior as the inability to adjust to ongoing or changing conditions. Generally the individual relies on both heredity and learning to cope with such alterations. Any set of circumstances producing conditions with which the individual is unable to cope can be called an ecological trap. As an example, Calhoun cites the lemming (Calhoun, 1967). Every three to four years the population of lemmings in arctic tundra regions becomes extremely dense. Often the crisis is solved by the sudden death of large numbers of animals. In some circumstances, however, vast migrations of the small animals occur. Over most arctic regions such migrations lead to eventual dispersal of population and individual death. In Scandinavia, however, the tundra is marked by long valleys extending to the sea. In these regions the migrations of the lemmings can take the form of huge aggregates of individuals that appear to have lost all behavioral restraints. The masses move continuously crossing everything in the path up to the sea itself. The water is no barrier, however, as the animals swim out into the sea until eventually all drown.

Such migrations into the sea cannot be explained solely by heredity. After all, the only survivors are the ones who do not exhibit the trait. Over time, therefore, one could presume natural selection would have removed the trait if it were hereditary. Calhoun believes that the particular configuration of the Scandinavian tundra forces the movement of the lemmings into a constant directionality reinforced in effect by the movement from high to low population density and requiring a long extinction period. Upon reaching the sea, the strongly implanted necessity to move ahead forces the animals into the water and on to their deaths.

In a carefully reasoned manner, Calhoun sought to subject his idea to experimental conditions. Focusing on a population of wild mice in a natural habitat, the experimenters sought to induce the movement of mice away from their established territories. In essence all the mice in a central area were removed by trapping. The belief was that mice on the perimeter of the central trapping area would become aware of the void and would automatically move into it to equalize the intensity of stimuli impinging from all sides. In effect, the experimenters would create an implosion of the mouse population, the opposite of the lemmings migration but based on the same principles. The experimenters caused four waves of mice to move into the central area, each more numerous than the preceding (Calhoun, 1967). The mice were caught in a set of circumstances to which they could not adjust; they were in an ecological trap.

The crowded universes also produced ecological traps. One of these, the behavioral sink, arose from observations of behavior as density increased. As used by Calhoun, the term *behavioral sink* refers to the process by which a population spread fairly evenly or uniformly across the space accessible to it becomes transformed into localized aggregates that far exceed optimal group size (Calhoun, 1967). As population rose, it happened that more than one animal would attempt to feed at the same time. Eating, therefore, came to be associated with the presence of another animal. Over time the animals tended to return to the same hopper, since the chance of encountering another increased. As population reached about three times the optimal, ever larger aggregates came to feed at the same hoppers, even though others were well-stocked and virtually ignored. The extreme crowding at the preferred hoppers led to levels and intensity of contact that resulted in impaired behavior in some animals. In general sexual and maternal behaviors deteriorated and aggressive behaviors increased. Over time as density continued to increase, individuals in great numbers became either very withdrawn or turned into what Calhoun called "the beautiful ones," mice who appeared to be in excellent health with fine pelage. These animals did not reproduce (Calhoun, 1962).

Much of Calhoun's work with crowding is based on a calculation of optimal group size, which for mammals varies by species from twelve to eighteen individuals. In general, twelve adults in a social group comprises the general tendency of mammalian evolution (Calhoun, 1977). Optimum group size is a product of heredity, experiential history, and environmental setting. When population density forces a degree of contact twice that of the optimum, the group will split into two. When density increases even further, pathology will appear.

Clearly human population has progressed far beyond that which would permit each individual to associate with approximately twelve adults. Calhoun attributes the ability of the human to move beyond the constraints of group size to the development of conceptual space or area. "Conceptual area amounts simply to the acquisition of values and codes which permit role differentiation to the extent that, even in a double-sized group in the original physical area, meaningful social contacts would continue at the rate necessary to maximize gratification" (Calhoun, 1971, p. 358). Calhoun believes conceptual space has increased as human population has increased.

Calhoun and MacLean are studying the mechanisms and outcomes of the "dance of life," the emotional system that governs much of animate life. That such an emotional system plays a role in human behavior appears indisputable, and it is only in the context of an emotional system, a dance of life, that Bowen Theory can be understood.

Calhoun and MacLean make clear the dilemma such automatic behavior produces. What originated in evolution as an adaptive mechanism to provide greater response and flexibility to the early mammal can limit adaptive capacity if pressed by too great a pressure to cope with a changing environment. Calhoun's notion of the ecological trap addresses this dilemma.

If, to this view of the emotional system, one adds the idea of individual variation in the ability to manage and retain adaptive flexibility, one arrives at a perspective analogous to the concept of differentiation, the cornerstone of Bowen Theory. The basic notion is that different organisms have differing ranges of tolerance to the demand to adapt. Such differences are a product of heredity and history. Once the tolerance level is surpassed, response becomes increasingly rigid and intense. If this state continues for an extended period of time, stress-induced changes can become irreversible.

In a sense Bowen Theory addresses the interplay of different levels of brain development as expressed in the behavior of the individual. The limbic functions, presumably an evolutionary development providing greater adaptive response and flexibility to the early mammal, can inhibit the functioning of a later evolutionary development, the neocortex. A key variable is the level of demand to adapt to a changing environment. The more the pressure to adapt, the greater the likelihood of the operation of automatic behaviors or mechanisms that hinder the full potential of neocortical functioning.

To see the dance of life, however, does not imply understanding. Yet unless one can see it, Bowen Family Systems Theory makes little sense. At the heart of Bowen Theory is the concept of the *system*. The remainder of this volume will essentially be concerned with defining and explaining this concept.

Specific systems are known to science. Astronomers refer to various systems of planets and stars. Medicine knows the cardiovascular system and other bodily systems. Yet the mind balks at the effort to comprehend systems. Words like *interdependence, mutual influence,* and so on are often used to catch the flavor of systems. Such terminology is inadequate, however, to convey more than a glimpse of the concept. Systems can best be observed with a broad focus. Bowen once likened it to looking at a football game from the roof of the stadium rather than from a seat on the fifty-yard line.

A significant element in that broad focus involves the continued effort to see the operation of natural systems. Systems operating principles are contained as much within the seed of a flower as within the vast herds of wildebeest on the African plain. Among the most important natural science research within which the nature of systems can be observed is the work of field biologists like George Schaller or Jane Goodall and of sociobiologists, most prominently E. O. Wilson. The system of an insect society or a lion pride is not the same as a human system. The point is to learn to recognize the characteristics of natural systems.

In the effort to study man, one can focus on human uniqueness, on how man differs from all other living things. Any effort that essentially takes as its object the productions of the human brain concerns itself with how humans are different from other life-forms. A second option, however, is to concern oneself with how man is like other living things. Biology is the study of life and living things, and the recognition of the similarity of life-forms was and is an important step in the process that produced the theory of evolution.

In a 1976 paper, Bowen highlighted a principal assumption that guided his work. "The theoretical assumption considers emotional illness to be a disorder of the *emotional system,* an intimate part of man's phylogenetic past which he shares with all lower forms of life, and which is governed by the same laws that govern all living things" (Bowen, 1976, pp. 59-60).

The great pressures or instincts that govern much of life are seen in the urge to survive and to engage in sexual activity leading to reproduction. In a static environment any organism could simply employ particular strategies to assure its own survival and reproduction, and there would be no need to evolve. There is, however, no such thing as a static environment. With the evolution of multicellular life-forms, the interplay of organisms became more complex, and greater adaptive flexibility was required.

Each organism that has ever lived possesses some sort of guidance system governing its efforts to survive and reproduce. Early forms obviously did not rely on anything like a brain or central nervous system. Simple chemical or electrical mechanisms may have served early living things much as they do many modern forms.

Within a particular environment each guidance system fits with every other. This is most clear in the predator-prey attachment or in mating behavior within a species. In a sense every organism is dependent on every other, even its enemies, to assure the efficient performance of its own guidance mechanisms. Should either predator or prey, for example, attain a new response it has a potential advantage if the new response furthers its own efforts to survive and reproduce. In short, every organism influences and is influenced by its environment and such interplay is necessary for the evolutionarily programmed behavior of the organism. Organism and environment evolve together.

Although this is a simple point, some examples may help illustrate the interplay of guidance systems in nature. Certain parasites of the phylum Acanthocephala (thorny-headed worms) have evolved a fascinating strategy that alters the guidance system of another organism (Moore, 1984). These worms infect an intermediary host, in this case the common pill bug, and alter the behavior of the bug in such a manner that it becomes an easy meal for the definitive prey, various birds in whose innards the parasite finally lodges.

Normally a secretive creature eschewing unsheltered and dry areas, the pill bug, when infected, appears to ignore available shelter and tends to be less averse to dry, light-colored areas than noninfected insects. Without shelter and exposed on a light background, the pill bug becomes an easy prey for scavenging birds. Moore also reports on the activity of another sort of parasite that affects the behavior of organisms in water, causing them to expose themselves to predation by various types of water fowl, thereby conveying the parasite to the definitive host.

A different sort of example comes from two dinosaur nesting sites in Montana (Horner, 1984). At these sites fossilized nests have been discovered with eggs and the remains of young dinosaurs still in place. These remains suggest that 80 million years ago certain herbivorous dinosaurs were evolving toward some sort of adult interaction with offspring. Among the dinosaur nests the investigators also found eggs laid in a straight line, quite unlike the circular, clearly constructed nests of the herbivores. These are the eggs of carnivorous dinosaurs, who are believed to have hatched within the nesting grounds where they could prey upon the young vegetarians. The interplay of the two dinosaur species presumably was shaping the instinctual behavior of each, the one toward parental care and the other toward enhanced predation. Horner's paper points to early evidence for the development of bonds between parent and offspring, an early harbinger of what has come to be called family.

With mammals, however, the development reached its greatest complexity. Modern man (*Homo sapiens sapiens*) is only the most recent version of a long evolutionary line. Modern man appeared on the planet between forty and fifty thousand years ago, quickly replacing his immediate predecessor, *Homo sapiens neanderthalenis* (Pilbeam, 1984).

With slight exceptions the evolution of homonoids and hominids has been marked by increasing brain size and, presumably, increasingly complex behavior. Kinship bonds within the living group, that is, family, has been a part of that evolution.

To state that family is a biological phenomenon is merely to note the obvious. It is as much a product of evolution as the migrations of the whales, the waggle dance of the honeybee, and the newborn calf's lurching steps toward the mother's nipple during the earliest moments of life. The roots of the family are very old indeed, perhaps as much as 250 million years to the evolution of the therapsids or mammal-like reptiles. The family is one manifestation of the human guidance system at work, and the family as a unit is a natural system.

Whether humankind has the ability to study and understand its own functioning remains to be seen. A major stumbling block is the tendency for each person to exclude self from the web of interconnectedness and automatic response that forms the dance of life. Human subjectivity defines self as different from all others. The challenge of systems is to understand on an emotional level one's connectedness to family, society, nature, and the earth and to guide oneself responsibly within that awareness.

References

Bertalanffy, L. von. (1968). *General system theory: foundations, development, applications.* New York: George Braziller.

Bowen, M. (1966). The use of family theory in clinical practice. *Comprehensive Psychiatry, 7,* 345-374.

Bowen, M. (1975). Family therapy after twenty years. In S. Arieti (Ed.), *American handbook of psychiatry: Volume 5. Treatment* (pp. 367-392). New York: Basic Books.

Bowen, M. (1976). Theory in the practice of psychotherapy. In P. Guerin (Ed.), *Family therapy: Theory and practice* (pp. 42-90). New York: Gardner Press.

Bowen M. (1982a, Winter). Mental health and science. *Newsletter of the American Family Therapy Association,* pp. 1-3.

Bowen, M. (1982b). Subjectivity, Homo sapiens and science. *The Family Center Report, 3*(2) 1-3.

Calhoun, J. B. (1956). A comparative study of the social behavior of two inbred strains of house mice. *Ecological Monographs, 26,* 81-103.

Calhoun, J. B. (1962). A behavioral sink. In E. Bliss (Ed.), *Roots of behavior* (pp. 295-315). New York: Paul Hoever.

Calhoun, J. B. (1963). *The ecology and sociology of the Norway rat.* (DHHS Publication No. 1008). Washington, DC: U.S. Government Printing Office.

Calhoun, J. B. (1967). Ecological factors in the development of behavioral anomalies. In *Comparative psychopathology* (pp. 1-51). New York: Grune & Stratton.

Calhoun, J. B. (1971). Space and the strategy of life. In A. H. Esser (Ed.), *Behavior and environment: The use of space by animals and men* (pp. 329-387). New York: Plenum.

Calhoun, J. B. (1974). Environmental design research and monitoring from an evolutionary perspective. *Man-Environment Systems, 4,* 3-28.

Calhoun, J. B. (1977). Looking backward from the beautiful ones. In W. R. Klemm, (Ed.), *Discovery processes in biology: A collection of autobiographies* (pp. 26-65). New York: Krieger.

Calhoun, J. B. (1977). Crowding and social velocity. In S. Arieti & G. Chyzanowski (Eds.), *New dimensions in psychiatry* (Vol. 2.) New York: John Wiley.

Greenberg, N., MacLean, P. D., & Ferguson, J. L. (1979). Role of the paleostriatum in species-typical display behavior of the lizard (*Anolis carolinensis*). *Brain Research, 172,* 229-241.

Horner, J. R. (1984). The nesting behavior of dinosaurs. *Scientific American, 250*(4), 103-137.

MacLean, P. D. (1958). The limbic system with respect to self-preservation and the preservation of the species. *The Journal of Nervous Mental Disease, 127,* 1-11.

MacLean, P. D. (1970). The triune brain, emotion and scientific bias. In F. O. Schutt (Ed.), *The neurosciences: Second study program* (pp. 336-349). New York: Rockefeller University Press.

MacLean, P. D. (1972). Cerebral evolution and emotional processes: New findings on the striatal complex. *Annals of the New York Academy of Sciences, 193,* 137-149.

MacLean, P. D. (1978). A mind of three minds: Educating the triune brain. *Yearbook of the National Society for the Study of Education* (pp. 308-342).

MacLean, P. D. (1982a). Evolution of the psychencephalon. *Zygon, 17,* 187-211.

MacLean, P. D. (1982b). On the origin and progressive evolution of the triune brain. In E. Armstrong & D. Falk (Eds.), *Primate brain evolution: Methods and concepts* (pp. 291-316). New York: Plenum.

Moore, J. (1984). Parasites that change the behavior of their host. *Scientific American, 250*(5), 108-115.

Murphy, M. R., MacLean, P. D., & Hamilton. S. C. (1981). Species-typical behavior of hamsters deprived from birth of the neocortex. *Science, 213,* 459-461.

Pilbeam, D. (1984). The descent of hominoids and homonids. *Scientific American, 250*(3), 84-96.

Chapter 2

The Family as a Unit

Earth's great oceans, atmosphere, and land have always formed an interactive whole. (The planet is believed to be about 4 billion years old.) When life emerged to become a fourth major component is not certain, but modern research has pushed the date backwards to a moment at least 3 billion years ago. Contemporary investigators use the term *biosphere* to refer to all living things on Earth and their environment.

The biosphere is flexible and fluid. Its components shift and move, adapting, adjusting, and responding to one another. The earth is never at rest, and the biosphere is never static. The atmosphere moves and changes. Its component gases shift and blend in ever-new and mostly consistent and stable ways. The land and the waters display similar fluctuations, again mostly within a stable and consistent range. Living things, too, are mostly consistent and stable.

From this perspective Earth is a system. A shift in any of its elements produces a response in others. The shift-response cycle can be minimal, affecting only a few things within a small area. It can also be global, altering the nature of the biosphere itself. As a result, the modern planet is different from the swirling amalgam of gas and molten metal that emerged from the formation of the solar system four or five billion years ago. It is different, too, from the planet that produced living things three to four billion years ago.

Living things have always had the capacity to influence their environment. The earliest atmosphere had little oxygen, which was toxic to the microbial life occupying Earth's niches (Margulis & Sagan, 1986). These living forms, essentially cells without nuclei, developed mechanisms to harness light and elements in the air and water to produce nutrients for themselves. In the process, prokaryotic cells, as modern scientists classify these organisms, released waste products. Among them was oxygen in sufficient quantities to change the basic composition of the atmosphere. Other microbes developed the ability to utilize these wastes. Clearly the interdependence of living things was established early in life's development.

Microbes remain the most abundant of living things. They occur in all environments known on Earth and are essential for the proper functioning of other living creatures. They live independently and in conjunction with other forms of life. Such cohabitation is sometimes peaceful and sometimes deadly. Between one and one-half and two billion years ago life took a second turn. A new kind of creature emerged that was radically different from the microbe. This new phenomenon was the nucleated cell or eukaryote.

So great is the gulf between prokaryotic and eukaryotic cells that some have called it the most important evolutionary development of all time (Margulis & Sagan, 1986). No one knows for sure how this development came about. One line of thinking suggests that the nucleated cell was produced when certain prokaryotic cells altered their predator-prey relationship and formed a cooperative alliance. Instead of destroying the prey, the predator became incorporated into it. The enemies merged and became interdependent. Each maintained some of its original capabilities and assumed a function necessary for the other. Such thought suggests that cooperation was at least as important as competition in the process of evolution. The nucleated cell is the basis of all complex organisms. All living things other than the microbes are formed from arrangements of nucleated cells cooperating with one another.

Eukaryotic and prokaryotic cells are naturally occurring systems. Like the biosphere of which it is a part, the cell is flexibly fluid. Its parts are functionally interdependent. Without each part of the cell fulfilling its function, the survival of the cell is jeopardized. A shift in the functioning of one part produces shifts in the functioning of other parts. Each element of the living cell has the capacity to influence the whole and to respond to the influence of elements outside itself.

The shifting fluidity of the cell's interior results in certain processes or behaviors that are recognizable when one focuses on the cell as a whole. For example, food is imported and by-products exported from the cell. A free-standing cell may move, altering is shape and its position relative to other parts of its environment. Reproduction occurs, replacing one cell with two identical ones, and so forth.

Although the cell is shifting fluidly in response to a myriad of internal and external cues, at any given moment its components have a particular interactional configuration or condition. This condition can be thought of as the *functional state* of the cell. The cell's capabilities for maintaining itself and for behavior are determined by its functional state. The notion of *health* is really one of functional state. A healthy cell has certain capabilities and options for behavior open to it which differ from those of a less healthy cell. A healthy cell behaves differently from an unhealthy one. The functional state of a cell may remain relatively stable over time, it may change slowly, or its condition may be rapidly altered. The functional state of a cell can be affected by factors within the cell itself and by interaction with its environment. In fact it is difficult if not impossible to separate these processes.

Organisms are composed of innumerable nucleated cells that have become specialized over time to create organs and perform specific functions within the system of cells. Like the cell, the organism is fluid, shifting, and mostly stable. The notion of the functional state is applicable to the organism as well as to the cell. Processes operate constantly, and the state of the organism is subject to continual variation. The component systems of the organism are also functionally interdependent. Each must perform in a particular way to allow the organism to maintain its health. Any variation affects the functional state of the organism and the well-being of any component.

Each cell and each organism operates in accordance with a built-in guidance mechanism. For example, in the developing embryo, all cells begin alike but ultimately differentiate to become highly specialized. An animal moving through a forest regularly changes gait, profile, and direction based on its perception of the environment and the processes that form its guidance system. A sunflower in a field orients its blossom regularly toward the sun. Clearly some sort of interplay between environment and the living unit triggers processes within the individual that lead to specific behaviors. Out of the scope of all possible behaviors, only a few appear at any given time. Furthermore, not all living things are capable of the same behaviors. For example, plant behavior differs in significant ways from animal behavior. Not all animals are capable of similar things. Some are more flexible than others, able to survive and even thrive under a range of environmental conditions.

The guidance system of the cell is basically biochemical. Chemical reactions are facilitated within and between the cell and its environment. Such reactions may alter the functional state of the cell. Some reactions occur regularly and repeatedly, forming the routine condition of the cell. Others occur rarely and represent basic shifts in the state or condition of the cell.

The interaction between cells is based in the biochemistry of each cell, but also involves the behavior of cells as entire units. How a cell behaves influences the cells with which it comes into contact. For example, the T-cells of the human immune system regularly patrol the body, alert to the presence of invading microbes. They identify cells as self or nonself basically by means of chemical processes. When a foreign presence is located, the T-cell moves aggressively upon the invader. The behavior of the T-cell has major implications for the cell with which it is in contact. Such interaction, therefore, is guided both by the processes within each cell and by the nature of the behavioral interaction. When a cell can influence another in an unexpected or unusual manner, something new occurs. The nature of the interaction changes. Such is the case, for example, between the AIDS virus and the cells of the immune system.

Such interactions determine the functional state and capabilities of organisms. The biochemistry of each cell within an organ determines its behavior. The behavior of each cell within the organ cluster of cells affects every other. How the cells interact together forms the behavior of the organ. The behavior of the organ affects other organ groups. The total biochemistry and behavior of cells, organ systems, and other components creates the behavior of the organism as an entity. Consequently the functioning of each cell underlies the functioning of all bodily components. Each component affects every other.

While all members of a species can be presumed to function in accordance with the same general guidance system, each particular individual differs from every other. One explanation for such diversity suggests that the basis of variance is genetic. Some individuals have genes that influence morphology and functioning in one direction, and some have genes that lead in another. A second explanation invokes experience of the individual as the basis for the variation.

When one considers the basis for individual variation as dichotomous (genes versus experience), one greatly oversimplifies an extremely complex arena. There seems no easy way to separate the two in the development and functioning of the individual. DNA clearly provides the blueprint for developing the materials and assembling the organism. If such development could be likened to the building of a prefabricated house, the genes would provide the foundation, the preformed sections of the house, and the general placement of the materials in relation to one another. They would also lay the basic electrical and piping systems of the structure. Experience — the retained effects of the interaction of the developing organism with its environment — also plays a part. In terms of the construction analogy, experience could be compared to the various craftsmen whose work renders a basic structure operational. The master electrician, trim carpenter, plumber, and so on all leave their mark on the finished house.

The evolutionary pathway leading to *Homo sapiens* produced a brain, a spinal column, and related peripheral nerve systems. There is a tendency to think of the central and peripheral nervous systems as the guidance system for the human. In a limited sense this is the case. The great neuronal net serves as a central coordinating and processing unit. Here signals of varying intensity from all over the organism are collected and processed. Some signals (for example the spinal reflex) undergo little processing while others follow complicated routes where they are modified in innumerable ways before a signal returns to a remote region of the body.

These great nerve networks are themselves a system with interdependent functioning. The central nervous system (CNS) is always active and shifting. Biochemical balances ebb and flow as hormones, neurotransmitters, and other molecules are released, taken up and held, or destroyed. Electrical activity shifts as nerve "circuits" become active or dormant. If the biochemicals could be imagined each to have a brilliant color and the electrical activity of the CNS could be likened to a network of lights, then the CNS would seem a work of abstract art with fascinating blends of everchanging color and winking lights of varying intensity.

The CNS, with its central coordinating role, must clearly be considered an influential component in the guidance system of the individual. But each cell and each organ system also contribute. Like medieval English monarchs who served as *primus inter pares*, the CNS may be first among equals. But its ascendancy is shaky, dependent upon the functioning of the other component elements of the organism.

Cells and organisms are fairly easily seen as units. They are, after all, self-contained within a boundary (the plasma membrane of the cell and the skin of the organism). Units larger than the individual organism where such a clear delineation is lacking are somewhat more difficult to comprehend. Nevertheless, such multi-individual units are the rule among the colonial invertebrates and the social insects (Wilson, 1975). Creatures like the Portuguese man-of-war, a colonial invertebrate well known to ocean bathers of the eastern United States, are colonies of individual organisms which have evolved together to function as a unit. Such colonies frequently display functional interdependence. The social insects form colonies as well. Ants and termites live in large groups of individuals that appear to have the behavior of a unit. Individuals assume functional tasks for the colony (soldier, worker, queen), and the individual has little capacity to survive outside the colonial structure.

Such colonies appear to be guided by a system of interactions among the individuals who comprise the colony. Each individual plays a part. The idea of the functional state applies to the aggregate as well as to the individual. For example, ant colonies rest, march, fight, and construct nests. Each activity could be seen as representing a functional state of the unit. That condition is shaped by the functioning of each individual and the clusters of individuals within the whole. Each organism contributes to the state of the unit and is influenced by that condition.

Unit functioning can be observed among many mammalian species as well. The behavior of each animal plays a part in the functional state of the group, and the behavior of the group impacts upon the well-being of each individual. Unit functioning is particularly evident in the defensive and hunting aggregates of many species.

Many mammals live in groups that are based loosely on kinship. Generally at the core of such groupings is the reproductive female. The group may be comprised of several such females and their appendages (mates and offspring). Within the group, various processes influence the overall condition of the assemblage and the behavior of each individual within it. For example, many primate groups display hierarchies. The males in the group occupy different social rankings determined to a large degree by the effect of individual differences on group interaction. Similar processes are evident among females as well. They affect the well-being of each individual both immediately and over time.

The human family displays the characteristics of a living system. The unit is flexible and fluid. For the family, the question is not whether individuals respond to one another, but how they respond. A shift in the functional state of the family is reflected in the state or condition of each individual organism. The shifts can be reflected behaviorally, or they may be contained within the body walls of the affected persons. The implications of such a view are far-reaching. Behavior may not be the only product of relationship. The health of each family member may be directly related to the functional state of the family unit.

The basic structure of the human family is descriptively contained within the term *nuclear family*. The term has become so commonplace that one tends to lose sight of its fundamental accuracy. It stems from the observation that families appear to have an emotional center or nucleus to which family members (and other nonrelated individuals) are responsively attached. From this viewpoint the family can be defined as the total number of individuals attached to an emotional nucleus.

The definition suggests a dual analogy. Atoms have nuclei around which attached particles whirl. Eukaryotic cells, from which all complex life forms are created, also have nuclei with which other components of the cell interact. Each is, however, an imperfect analogy for the nuclear family. There is a certain appeal in comparing the nuclear family to the atom. The family center seems to exert pressure on the individuals attached to it. The nature of the family can change as component members are added or subtracted. The changes can be smooth or energetic. Similar things can be said to apply to the atom. The precise nature of the pressures or forces that hold the family together, however, remains elusive. The clarity of measurable electromagnetic forces that apply to the atom cannot be replicated in the family. One can say only that family members act as if they are attached to one another.

The eukaryotic cell, on the other hand, is a living unit. Its component elements are functionally interdependent and form a guidance system for the unit. The cell is a self-contained unit, and the family, at least overtly, is not. The analogy holds rather well, however, between the cell and the multicellular organism. The latter is essentially a composite of eukaryotic cells that are genetically identical but have differentiated to perform various functions necessary to the maintenance of the organism as a whole. The cells and the organ systems they form are functionally interdependent, and the organism is contained within a membranous barrier.

The term *emotion* or *emotional* as used in the definition of nuclear family given above requires further clarification. Darwin used the term to address underlying aspects of human and animal behavior that were broader than a single human culture and were evident across species. For example, certain facial configurations accompany internal states for people. Individuals from one culture easily recognize the look and identify the internal state represented simply on the basis of photographs of people from another quite different culture. Similarly, the manifestations of illness are universal. Such signs can be considered emotional. The external manifestations of emotion have a dual function. They signal an internal state and have a communicative function to other individuals.

In a broad sense, *emotion* can refer to all processes that guide the individual automatically within an environment. Emotion would include genetic factors, experientially acquired mechanisms, and the functional state of the unit at the moment in question. For example, all living things must somehow acquire nutrients. How they behave is, to a large extent, directed by the mandate to eat or be eaten. The functional state of the individual determines the immediate behavior, and the constant requirement to obtain food determines broad movements or patterns over time. For example, when an organism feeds and rests is influenced by its functional state. When it migrates or establishes a territory is also a product of the animal's functional state shifting in response to environmental conditions. Such organization of immediate and long-term behavior can appropriately be called emotional.

The evolution of sexual reproduction opened another emotional arena. Males and females orient themselves toward one another, at least some of the time, and toward others of either sex who are seen as competitors. In addition, at least for some species, infants spend a portion of their development literally attached to their mothers and an additional, longer period of time in a dependent status upon a caretaker, generally but not necessarily the mother.

Humans have apparently always formed units of parent and offspring. Other caretakers can be substituted, but the human organism seems to strive toward the parent-child unit whenever possible. It is, seemingly, a part of the human emotional system. The process begins with a breeding pair.

One is tempted to call the breeding pair the emotional nucleus of the family. This is the case for large numbers of people. But many families exist composed of a single parent and attached offspring. There are also examples, such as adoption, where families are formed around adults who act as caretakers for children to whom they have no genetic relationship. Such units appear to function as well as those formed from a breeding pair.

From this perspective, therefore, the primary caretaker of the young is seen as the emotional nucleus or center of the family. This role is inescapably filled by the mother during the child's intrauterine development. After birth, other possibilities exist. Generally speaking, however, the mother continues to serve this function across her lifetime. Said somewhat differently, the breeding female is the principal component of an emotional nucleus. After the birth of the infant, others may take over that function partially or totally, although the mother tends to maintain it herself, all things being equal.

The breeding male is clearly required for human reproduction, but his role in the emotional nucleus of the family is much less fixed. While his presence may be limited only to copulation, there is clearly a tendency for the breeding male to become an element in the emotional nucleus. The interplay between the breeding pair greatly influences the functional state of the family as a unit.

The term *attachment* is frequently used to refer to the relationship between male and female, parent and child. While they are not overtly bound together, individuals act as if their behavior is linked to that of others. The breeding pair initially creates a habitat together, frequently before pregnancy results and generally rapidly after impregnation. With the creation of the habitat they also tend to divide tasks related to its maintenance and to their continued survival as a unit. In this sense, that of task division and survival, the male and female tend to become dependent upon one another. When one fails to function with regard to a common task, the other pays a price of some sort.

Were this interlocking of tasks the only mechanism of attachment between male and female, they could separate relatively easily by reclaiming for oneself tasks assumed by the other. Some disruption of functioning might occur for each, but generally the separation could be accomplished relatively easily. Variables that might affect the separation could include the length of time of the interdependency and the degree to which tasks had become separated into exclusive domains of each. The experience of each in functioning independently prior to attachment would presumably also be of importance.

The linking of male and female in a breeding pair clearly has more to it than the simple exchange of tasks and responsibilities. The process leading to reproduction generally begins with a condition generally known as "falling" or "being in love." In this state each individual experiences feelings of personal well-being. Communication between male and female is open and relatively effortless. When "in love," people can also display a narrowness of vision and a blindness to dilemmas that seem obvious to the noninvolved observer.

The state or condition of "being in love" appears to involve processes within each individual on a very deep or complex level. It represents a major shift in the functional state of the organism. More than a psychological process, falling in love is an organismic experience. The changes in perception and behavior suggest clearly that biochemical changes are occurring and internal processes are altering themselves at least temporarily. The capacity to fall in love is within the emotional system of the organism.

Lehrman's (1964) study of ring doves provides one examle of how an innate capability might come to be played out in a particular environment. No claim could be made that the processes or the ring dove are homologous to those of the human. Nevertheless, on the level of analogy, the birds are quite informative.

The reproductive cycle of behavior for the male and female ring dove involves specific changes in behavior over the course of the cycle. A complicated interplay between psychology and biology is involved. The entire cycle lasts about six weeks, moving through phases of courtship, selection of a nest site, nest-building, copulation, egg-laying, incubation, and the production of crop-milk, a liquid secretion produced in the bird's crop on which the young feed. After about six weeks, the cycle is complete, the young are more or less launched, and the courting begins once again.

Each step in this process is accompanied by behavioral and physiological changes. For example, crop growth could be eliminated in males if the bird were removed from the nest before crop development began. If, however, the male were removed but placed in an adjacent cage separated from the nesting female by a transparent partition, crop growth would continue as if the male were actually participating in the incubation. Simply seeing the incubating female precipitates processes in the male leading to glandular activity altering the bird's physiology. In a similar vein, Lehrman was able to demonstrate that ovarian development in a similarly isolated female occurred providing she could see a male performing in the manner of courtship.

Lehrman's results pointed to a subtle and complex relationship between external stimuli from the environment leading to endocrinal changes within the individual and the effects of such hormonal activity on the behavior of the individual. Two sets of reciprocal interrelations seem to be operative: (1) the effects of hormonal secretions on behavior and the effects of external stimuli, including the behavior of the animal itself, on hormonal secretion and (2) the effects of the presence and behavior of one mate on the endocrinal system of the other and vice versa.

To the degree that such processes occur in the human, people become reciprocally responsive to one another acting in certain ways. The nature of the response is emotional in nature and affects the entire organism. Such interdependency can develop as a result of intense processes between individuals. The processes referred to as parent-infant bonding or falling in love, for example, lead to an interpersonal interlock, marked by preferential sensitivity and responsiveness, and the process known as grief may represent the adjustment of a person to the dissolution of such an interactional structure.

These processes would be marked by changes in the entire organism. They could be considered to be coded in the emotional system of the individual and expressed behaviorally when the functional state of the organism is appropriate. It may be that individuals are more or less receptive to such processes at certain developmental stages or windows. They could take place at any time, but certain periods would be more favorable than others. In addition, other factors may contribute to the process. Exposure to one another frequently over time may be a factor. Repeated sexual activity, occupying the same space (particularly sleeping in the same bed or in close proximity to one another), and joint exposure to anxiety-arousing situations in which one or both perceives the other as essential to personal well-being or even survival may play a role. The processes of pregnancy, birth, and parenting as they affect each person also are influential.

Clearly human breeding pairs form an attachment or linkage of the general sort described above. It is a natural process. But not all mates link with one another to the same degree. Said somewhat differently, the functional state of each is influenced by the behavior of the other to a greater or lesser degree. Not all breeding pairs are alike in terms of the degree of linkage. The greater the degree of attachment or linkage, the greater the sensitivity of each to the other as manifested in the functional state of the individual and in the behavior of the breeding pair.

Shifts in the functional state of the individual can be noted in two general areas — the physical functioning of the organism and the mental activity of the individual. Shifts in physical functioning are often subtle and not easily noticed without measuring instrumentation and training. The most obvious physical responses fall within the general area of anxiety and can be measured by the equipment of the biofeedback laboratory. In response to the presence or absence of the partner (or even to thoughts about the partner) changes in heart rate, blood pressure, muscle tension, and so forth can be observed. Presumably other changes may also occur in some people in systems and processes within the organism that are not easily measured by noninvasive procedures.

Shifts in mental activity can also be noted both in the nature of the process itself and in the content of which the individual can be aware. Shifts in the process of mental activity include the speed of mental activity, for example, either a slowing down or a speeding up of mental processes; the breadth of perception, such as the inability to discriminate among stimuli or the exclusive focus on a limited number of stimuli; and in the feeling tone that accompanies the activity. Content shifts can run the gamut from that which would normally be considered psychotic to planful and responsible intellectual activity.

The behavior of the breeding pair also provides information as to the degree of attachment. In a general sense attachment can be noted in the tolerance of each for difference in the other and the measures which are brought into play when such tolerance is exceeded. In pairs intensely linked together, great efforts are made to minimize the appearance of difference between the participants. Male and female may dress alike, engage exclusively in the same activities, present to others the appearance of thinking alike about all subjects, and carefully work to avoid all environmental and interpersonal interactions that might introduce difference. When differences arise in such pairs (as they almost certainly will), the participants will go to great lengths to reestablish the sameness. Each may attempt to persuade or even force the other to give up the perceived difference. Or one may eliminate his or her own view or behavior in order to fit better with the change in the other. When the difference cannot be eliminated, severe conflict may erupt or even the abrupt dissolution of the breeding unit. The effort to maintain or reestablish can become so intense that much of the time and energy of the pair goes toward maintenance with a corresponding slump functioning in other areas of life. Less intensely attached pairs display greater tolerances for difference and direct more of their personal energy and resources to the attainment of other objectives outside of the breeding unit.

The basic nuclear family structure is complete when a child is produced by the breeding pair. Arising out of the linking of parental gametes, each infant begins life firmly attached to its mother. The developmental process of the infant can be described as one of increasing ability to function for oneself. The resolution of direct attachment to mother is achieved at birth. The resolution of emotional attachment is the task of subsequent years of development. How the parents or primary caretakers have progressed in their own developmental efforts is believed directly to effect their child's ability to attain functional independence.

While the basic structure of the person-to-be is incorporated in the genome, much finishing work remains. Experience — defined as the retained effects of the interaction of the developing organism with its environment — accounts for the further refinement of the individual. There can, of course, be differences in the basic genome which then influence the further development of the organism. Environmental factors may influence the impact of such differences, but the basic plan will unfold. Down's syndrome, for example, represents the unfolding of a genetic plan critically different from standard at a single chromosome.

The initial environment with which the embryo must contend is the uterus of its own mother. This is primarily a chemical environment, where subtle shifts in the balance of the mother's biochemistry are reflected in the fetus. The mother's ingestion of chemical substances can have severe consequences. Fetal alcohol syndrome is an example. The mother's nutritional state at certain fetal developmental points is also highly influential. Other aspects of the mother's functional state may have developmental consequences for her infant.

The functional state of the mother is, at least partially, the product of her responsiveness to the environment in which she finds herself. An important element in the environment is her mate. Based on her degree of attachment to that male, the mother's functional state can shift frequently and/or dramatically in response to her perception of his behavior. Since he, in turn, also responds to her, an emotional field is created between them that can influence the environment of the embryo and thus embryonic development.

The interplay between the functional states of the mother and of the infant has a nine-month history at the time of birth. The arrival of the infant leads to a process extending and possibly intensifying the the linking of mother and child. The mother's role as caretaker is behaviorally more direct and not simply a matter of tending to her own health and well-being. Visual, olfactory, tactile, and auditory cues are experienced by each directly and processes or patterns of responsiveness rapidly develop.

The extension of attachment between mother and infant is complete shortly after birth with the two fully sensitized and responsive to one another. A similar, parallel process occurs with the father or other primary caretaker shortly after the infant's birth. In one sense, the mother is dispensable with the birth of the child. She can be replaced with a substitute caretaker who can fulfill the maternal role adequately. Mothers tend to retain the role of primary caretaker to their children, however, in almost all human environments. The speed, nature, and intensity of the attachment to a nonmaternal caretaker is influenced by that individual's exposure to the infant and the mother's tolerance for the involvement of the other with her child.

In the unit of breeding pair and child, the infant quickly develops responsiveness to each parent. The infant appears to be more sensitive initially to its mother. This implies that the infant has both a direct experience of another caretaker and a direct experience of the mother's reactivity to that other person. In other words, the infant has the direct perception of the other adult and its own sensitivity to shifts in maternal functional state which occur in the presence of the other individual. In the basic unit of two parents and a child, therefore, three interlocking attachments are at work at any given moment — that of the breeding pair and of each parent with the child. Each relationship can influence every other through the mechanism of shifts in functional state in each individual and the responsiveness of the others to those shifts.

This basic unit of the nuclear family is replicated as each additional child is added. The nuclear family can be described, therefore, as a series of interlocking triangles. Through such an interactional and responsive network of triangles, a shift in a particular individual or in a relationship can spread to affect the functional state and subsequently the behavior of others in the family. What affects any individual, therefore, can affect the whole, and what affects the whole can affect any individual.

The basic configuration of parents and child — a primary triangle — is alive with emotional activity. The functional state of each shifts constantly, and behaviors change frequently. The developmental path of the unit is characterized by the developing ability of each party to be responsible for self. For the neonate such a progression is obvious. Gradually the youngster comes to feed self, crawl, walk, and then run without assistance and to explore an ever-widening environment. Mental development follows a similar progression marked by increasing awareness and the development of the ability to reason and to make increasingly complicated decisions for self.

What is less obvious is that the primary caretakers are involved in a similar process. From the initial state of being totally responsible for the infant's well-being and survival, each caretaker slowly moves toward the ability to contain the urge to do for the youngster and to allow him or her to assume increasingly responsibility for self. That this is a lengthy process spread out across years is clear. It requires of the caretaker the ability to manage functional states in self that urge involvement with the youngster and to allow the child a similar opportunity to learn to manage self. Where the caretaker is unable to accomplish this task, the development of the child is hindered or blocked. As a result of such a blockage, the child does not become as independent as he or she potentially can be and remains attached or locked to the primary triangle. Development is incomplete.

Such a blockage or limitation is of theoretical importance. To the degree that responsibility for self is not attained, a need for another is established. This need for another governs the degree to which the individual attaches to others throughout life. In addition, the inability of the caretakers and child to evolve toward independence establishes in the child a sensitivity to the functional state of each parent and a corresponding functional state in self that is the basis for a reactive behavior in the person and in the unit. This set of relationships to caretakers, established in the primary triangle, becomes a template for future relationships of equal intensity, generally with mate and off-spring. Said somewhat differently, all future relationships become variations on a theme.

The emotional need for another can be described as incomplete separation of individuals or unfinished, partial differentiation of self. The incomplete differentiation of caretakers and child is handled in a number of ways that ignore the basic developmental problem. The outcome is a series of maneuvers to manage the difficulty the attachment generates. The unit can remain in lifelong reactive contact or the parties may break contact with one another and attempt to manage need for another elsewhere. No matter where the person turns, however, the need for another arises along with the sensitivity and reactivity that accompanies it.

What emerges from this view of family is a constellation of nuclear families across generations linked by the incomplete differentiation of the people involved. Each breeding pair is linked to the nuclear families that produced the male and female. The person appears to remain sensitive and responsive to events that alter the functional state of the primary triangle and of the nuclear family in which one was born and raised. Such reactivity can produce disruption in the breeding pair and thus in the nuclear family of a succeeding generation. In addition, each partner's need for another, brought from the original nuclear family, places constraints upon the autonomy of each partner and upon the flexibility of the new unit. Limitations in flexibility and autonomy impinge upon parenting ability and the capacity of the unit to adapt effectively to changing conditions.

Each nuclear family, therefore, is the endpoint of countless nuclear families before it. It is also a way station of human reproduction en route to other future generations of nuclear families. Each nuclear family is a unit, as is the broader, multigenerational constellation of nuclear families to which it belongs. The emotional need for another, established in each individual in each nuclear family but the product of countless generations, links each generation to its past while at the same time it influences the future. It is against this background of the family as a unit that Bowen Family Systems Theory takes shape.

References

Lehrman, D. S. (1964). The reproductive behavior of ring doves. *Scientific American, 211*(5), 82-88.

Margulis, L., & Sagan, D. (1986). *Microcosmos.* New York: Summit Books.

Wilson, E. O. (1975). *Sociobiology: The new synthesis.* Cambridge: Harvard University Press.

Chapter 3

Bowen Family Systems Theory

Bowen Family Systems Theory, or simply the Bowen Theory, consists currently of eight interlocking concepts. It is the product of years of observational research involving scores of families with a broad range of problems. First at the Menninger Clinic, then at NIMH, and currently at Georgetown University, Bowen has worked to understand the processes that govern human behavior.

Although his name is often connected with the study of schizophrenia, Bowen's initial interest was the attachment or symbiosis between mother and child, which he had observed in his clinical work. With his move to NIMH in 1954, various practical considerations led to schizophrenia as the laboratory within which to pursue the investigations of attachment. In his initial NIMH project, Bowen brought mothers and their dysfunctional offspring into the hospital setting. In an early paper, Bowen described the thinking behind the project. "The original hypothesis was based on a premise that the basic character problem, on which clinical schizophrenia is later superimposed, is an unresolved symbiotic attachment to the mother. It considered psychological symbiosis to be the same order of phenomenon as biological symbiosis" (Bowen, Dysinger, Brady, & Basmania, 1978, p. 4).

In this formulation several important assumptions are evident. The dysfunction in the child was viewed as a product of the attachment between mother and child and not solely as a pathological process within the individual. The term *symbiosis* highlights the mutuality of the process. The attachment is seen as a natural development that neither wants and for which neither could be blamed.

For this original NIMH project Bowen selected three chronically schizophrenic young women and their mothers. Selection was based more on the intensity of the attachment between mother and daughter than on the severity of symptomatology. The young women were housed on a NIMH research ward. The mothers could choose their degree of involvement. They could live on the ward with their offspring or live elsewhere and spend the day on the ward. By the end of the first year, the project was expanded to include entire families. The focus on the nature of the symbiosis had not changed. But Bowen's observations led him to the realization that the relationship between mother and daughter was part of a larger, fluctuating unit (Bowen et al., 1978).

The ability to see the family as an emotional unit or system and the symptoms in an individual as an element in the emotional functioning of that unit was a major step forward. In the family unit everyone plays a role. This is a difficult idea for most people to grasp. In an anxious environment it is much easier to see the problem in another and to miss the part self plays. Mental-health professionals generally have great difficulty seeing beyond what they have been trained to see as psychopathology within the individual.

The staff of the NIMH research ward ran into this difficulty. Clinicians were having trouble seeing beyond what their training led them to see. To move beyond this roadblock, the staff worked to avoid using conventional clinical terminology. The goal was to describe what they saw in simple descriptive language. While this sort of exercise does not guarantee the ability to see the family as a unit, it does help clear the observer of preconceived ideas that hamper accurate observation.

In their efforts to see and interact with the family as the unit of illness rather than the individual, the staff moved through three levels of awareness (Bowen, 1961). Intellectual awareness of the family as a unit came quickly. Essentially this amounted to being able to understand the ideas involved. Clinical awareness, that is, implementing the ideas in clinical practice, was significantly more difficult. It was second nature for the staff to think primarily of the individual, and clinical work could easily fall back into an individual frame of reference. Bowen called the third level *emotional awareness*. On this plane staff members could begin to detach from overinvolvement and overidentification with a family member and could understand more fully the complexity of the family problem.

Several observations from the NIMH project were extremely important. The role of anxiety in family functioning became clear. Relationship could both produce and alleviate anxiety, and the effects could be observed in fluid patterns of involvement. A basic pattern concerns the closeness – distance cycle (Bowen et al., 1978). During the close phase, mother and daughter were interested mainly in each other. As closeness increased, anxiety was produced which led to conflict and separation. At some point, however, the distance between them generated its own anxiety, reversing the cycle back toward closeness.

The relationship of each to outsiders depended upon the stage or phase of the cycle. During the closeness phase, relationships to outsiders were calm. During the distanced phase, each appeared to attempt to establish intense involvements with outsiders. These intense relationship efforts were difficult and demanding for the outsiders involved.

Another important observation noted the degree to which the staff became involved in the emotional processes of the family. Anxiety could spread from the family and result in turmoil among the staff. At such times the family would be relatively free of anxiety (Bowen et al., 1978). The aroused staff members lost objectivity and functioned less effectively in their clinical activities. A related observation concerned the progress made by "research" families. These families, where the focus was on observation and the researcher was relatively free of emotional attachment, made better progress than families in which the focus was on psychotherapeutic intervention (Bowen, 1966).

The idea of functioning position also is rooted in those early observations. The concept is best conveyed through analogy. Bowen illustrates it with comparison to a football team (Bowen, Dysinger, & Basmania, 1959). One can look at the individual talents and skills of the players and make some prediction about the performance of a team. As all football fans know, however, many excellent, talented athletes play for losing teams. If one could observe the team from the top of the stadium or from an airborne camera, it would become clear that each of the eleven players has a function to perform or occupies a functioning position. The success of the team depends upon the performance of those interdependent functions and the operation of the team as a unit. Kerr (1981) uses the analogy of an engine to illustrate functioning position. If a person without mechanical experience were given a carburetor he or she could describe it in detail but would be hard-pressed to explain what it does. On the other hand, if the person were presented an engine missing only the carburetor, he or she could study the engine and design a piece that would perform the functions of the carburetor.

Each of the analogies is based on a broad perspective. The football player or the carburetor alone conveys little about the functioning position each occupies. Functioning position becomes clear only when an individual or piece is seen in relationship to all other individuals or pieces that comprise the unit. This is much easier to do when one studies an engine than a football team. It is even more difficult when one is attempting to see one's own functioning position in a family.

Functioning position is subject to change. When functioning positions change, the nature of the unit and its level of functioning is altered. Bowen (1959) describes the shifts in functioning in a family unit comprised of father, mother, and psychotic daughter. When the father was able to become more self-assertive, the mother's functioning appeared initially to decline. After a brief period she became calmer and more objective than previously. At that point, with the father and mother more involved with each other than with the daughter and more objective about her situation, the daughter began to make significant improvements in functioning.

Once patterns of emotional process could be seen in the research families, it became possible to see them in other, less impaired families as well. Bowen came to see the difference between psychosis and neurosis as quantitative rather than qualitative (Bowen, 1971). The emotional processes were essentially similar, and the major delineating factor between psychosis and neurosis was degree of impairment. Human functioning could be placed on a continuum from the poorest to the highest, a major variable being the intensity or pressures that propelled the process. This sort of continuum led to the concept of a scale of differentiation (Kerr, 1981).

In 1959 Bowen moved from the NIMH to Georgetown University. His thinking was ranging far beyond schizophrenia, although the publications of that period reflect commitments to the research project. The initial six concepts of Bowen Theory evolved rapidly between 1957 and 1963. Five of the concepts Bowen formulated directly. The sixth took shape with the fortuitous appearance of a book that gave shape to a line of thinking Bowen had not yet fully worked out. In 1961 Walter Toman published the first edition of his book *Family Constellation: A Psychological Game*. This provided the basis for the concept of sibling position. The original six concepts were formally presented as Family Systems Theory in 1966. The six concepts are triangles, nuclear family emotional process, family projection process, multigenerational transmission process, scale of differentiation and sibling position. In 1974 Bowen added his name to the Theory along with two additional concepts, emotional cutoff and emotional process in society.

Before directly presenting the eight concepts of Bowen Family Systems Theory, it is important to address once again the idea of emotion and the emotional system taken up in the first chapter. The modern human is a product of millions of years of evolutionary development. The human brain with its myriad of connections to the human body appears to be the center of a highly evolved guidance system, possibly the most complex ever to evolve. Rooted in protoplasm, the emotional system is the legacy of man's evolutionary past and a common denominator with other living forms. Bowen discusses his view of the emotional system in the following manner. "I view emotional illness as a much deeper phenomenon than that conceptualized by current psychological theory. There are emotional mechanisms as automatic as a reflex and that occur as predictably as the force that causes the sunflower to keep its face toward the sun" (Bowen, 1966, p. 354). The affects referred to by MacLean, particularly those described as general, may represent a meeting point of the emotional system with the cognitive system.

In this chapter the word intensity will appear frequently to refer to an interaction and to a level of anxiety. Feeling states can pass between and among organisms with great speed. The means of transmission are often subtle and may not involve language. Visual cues are important as well as voice tone and other more subtle sensory processes. The feeling states produced vary from the mild to the very strong. When *intensity* is used in reference to an interaction, it denotes feeling states produced in one or more individuals that move toward the very strong end of the continuum. It also addresses the speed of transmission between individuals. An intense interaction is one in which strong feeling states are produced and very rapidly transmitted among the participants to the exchange. Intense anxiety is a strong fear of real or imagined events. The more intense an interaction, the greater the likelihood that individuals involved will behave automatically, that is, in response to the emotional system with the intellectual system being overridden. When the term is applied to a relationship, in addition to the variables described above, it refers to the preoccupation of each party to the relationship with the other involved parties.

A major pathway of emotional expression is found in relationship. The principles that govern emotional functioning in relationship are believed to be orderly and knowable. The seed of the sunflower contains the complete operational program of a natural system. The seed develops or remains dormant in response to a variety of internal and external conditions. As any gardener knows, the seed lives in a continual exchange with its environment in predictable ways. It is difficult to say why the sunflower exists, but how it exists (or ceases to exist) is knowable. It is easier to observe the sunflower than the human. The closer man comes to himself, the cloudier his vision becomes. The tendency for each person to view him- or herself as an exception to the natural processes of living things is strong. One may see the connectedness of others but believe that self is different and autonomous.

Yet the human, possibly alone in the chain of living forms, may have the capacity to become somewhat objective about self. A person may be able to understand his or her own connectedness to others in the family, that of the family to society, and that of the human race to all other life and to the planet itself. It is not possible to develop the promise of Bowen Theory without the effort to acquire an operational level of objectivity, at least enough to recognize one's own subjectivity. To understand systems is to understand one's own emotional responsiveness to and functional position in the family and groups to which one belongs. The fundamental question from this perspective is not why man exists but how man functions.

Clearly human behavior is not completely automatic and emotional in the sense described above. At times people can plan on the basis of careful thought and some degree of assessment of external reality. Some people are able to do this much of the time, others very infrequently. A major variable affecting whether behavior will be guided emotionally or intellectually is the intensity of anxiety in the organism and the group.

Anxiety can be defined as the arousal of the organism upon perceiving a real or imagined threat. When so aroused, the emotional system of the anxious individual tends to override the cognitive system and behavior becomes increasingly automatic. Subjective decisions based on internal feeling or affect predominate. People tend to act to relieve discomfort, even though their decisions and behavior may lead to long-range difficulties and even greater discomfort. This is most clear in the extreme forms, for example the detoxified drinker whose urge to drink overpowers the knowledge of the effects of alcohol upon self. Yet anyone, when sufficiently anxious and uncomfortable, may automatically seek relief through some sort of behavior with complete disregard for the long-term consequences of such activity.

Bowen used the term *emotional reactivity* or *emotional reflex* to refer to such automatic response. Generally the automatic emotional response operates outside of a person's conscious awareness. Like a physical reflex, however, it can be observed and controlled to a degree. The emotional reflex can best be observed in a relationship with a moderate degree of anxiety. Too little anxiety reduces the reflex to a subtle level that is difficult to observe. In a highly charged situation the complexity of the automatic responses borders upon chaos.

Any relationship has its own variations and patterns. An example may help illustrate the point. A working wife encounters a situation in the office that raises her anxiety. She telephones her husband, basically seeking contact as a means to regain her equilibrium. As he answers the phone, the husband hears a note in his wife's tone of voice that he associates with anxiety in her. His stomach begins to tighten, and he has difficulty knowing what to say to her. She notes his hesitation and voice tone. She comments that she just wishes sometime that they could communicate without his becoming silent. What began as a problem at work ends as a relationship problem. This sort of action and reaction syndrome appears characteristic of interaction between organisms on many levels. The emotional reaction need not always be conflictual. It plays an important role in sexual behavior and is a common aspect of life.

It seems likely that humans have always lived in groups. Man's closest primate relative, the chimpanzee, also lives in a troop. Biological factors rooted in evolution continue to move the individual into a group. These factors are analogous to those at work in the ungulate herds of the Serengeti or in the smaller bands of the mountain gorilla. The grouping phenomenon seems particularly active in the presence of threat.

Bowen observed the human tendency to group together and called it the "togetherness force" (Bowen, 1971). When anxiety pervades a family, the tendency toward togetherness is most observable. The family describes all members as alike in terms of thoughts, principles, and feelings. Family members think and act as if they were responsible for the happiness, comfort, and well-being of the others. Some rebel and define themselves in a manner opposite to the others. The family is blamed for personal failures.

As tension or anxiety mounts, the manifestations of togetherness and loss of individuality increase. The feeling climate can be positive or negative. Within the family, relationships may be both positive and negative. Rebellion is a common reactive posture. Although the person generally denies the family's role, he or she sets a course that is the mirror opposite of that expected by the family. Another individual may comply totally with the family's emotional demands. Each of these postures relates to the pressures for group cohesion and sameness in the family. The higher the level of chronic anxiety in the family, the more each individual life course comes to be determined by various reactive mechanisms.

The togetherness force must be seen as natural and a necessary part of life. It exists together with a companion "force" or tendency for the person to be a separate and self-contained individual. When anxiety is low, family members automatically display autonomy. The person assumes greater responsibility for personal happiness and the decisions that shape a life course. Thinking and principles play a greater role than automatic processes in guiding behavior.

Paradoxically, the more an individual responds to pressures toward togetherness, the more he or she focuses on others and their impact on self. One notes where others are wrong, demanding, threatening, or loving and responds automatically. Other people are defined in terms of the relationship to self. Eventually the individual reacts as if he or she were the center of the universe, the star around which the family system revolved. In contrast a person who is more objective about the movement toward togetherness can see more clearly the role of one's own functioning and behavior in the family as a unit and the impact of one's behavior on others. The autonomous individual has a greater awareness of self as a responding element in a network and has less tendency to attribute undue importance to self.

The balance of pressures for togetherness and individuation within a person and a family shapes the life course of those involved. When anxiety leads to a new level of togetherness within a family, differentiation decreases as well, rendering the family less able to withstand heightened anxiety in the future. The movement toward greater individuation in a family appears to produce increased autonomy and reduced anxiety in the family unit. Bowen suggests that optimal functioning occurs when the forces are evenly balanced with neither overriding the other. Under such circumstances the family unit has sufficient flexibility to adapt to change.

If one envisioned a continuum with undifferentiation at one end and autonomy at the other, one would have a scale along which anyone could be placed on the basis of personal functioning. When anxiety is high, people tend to respond emotionally to the family unit and display greater undifferentiation. With reduced anxiety, increased autonomy becomes evident. Some families reveal chronic levels of anxiety. Members of such families tend to be more focused on the family group than on individuation. Yet even in these families some people are less caught up in the emotional processes of the family than others. They are more objective and less reactive than their relatives. Such people are valuable to the family and important to the process of family therapy.

A surge of anxiety in a family emotional unit reveals pressures both toward togetherness and individuation. Togetherness operates in the name of love, kinship, and loyalty. Individuation speaks of personal responsibility, self-determination, and personal principles. If greater togetherness prevails, the family moves toward increased emotional functioning and less individual autonomy. A by-product is increased chronic anxiety. If the family moves toward greater individuation, anxiety decreases. The balance of togetherness and individuation in a family is important. Bowen Theory indicates that families with a high degree of togetherness or undifferentiation are vulnerable to the development of major life problems (Bowen, 1966).

Bowen Family System Theory is comprised currently of eight concepts. With these concepts a coherent story of the functioning of a particular family across time can be told. The term *theory* contains within it the assumption that such propositions represent the best current thinking about the phenomenon, an established framework within which known facts can be explained. From such theoretical thinking comes all therapeutic methodology. The initial six concepts of Bowen Theory (differentiation of self, triangles, nuclear family emotional process, family projection process, multigenerational transmission process, and sibling position) were defined with sufficient clarity by 1963 that Bowen used the title Family Systems Theory to refer to them (Kerr, 1981). The seventh and eighth concepts (emotional cutoff and emotional process in society) were added in 1976. In the following pages each of the eight concepts will be discussed in detail.

DIFFERENTIATION OF SELF

The concept of differentiation of self is the core of Bowen Family Systems Theory. No other concept in Bowen Family Systems Theory is so often discussed and associated with Bowen's work. Differentiation concerns the individual. It addresses how people differ from one another in terms of their sensitivity to one another and their varying abilities to preserve a degree of autonomony in the face of pressures for togetherness.

It is difficult, if not impossible, to understand the concept of differentiation of self without seeing the family as an emotional unit. *Emotional* in this context refers to forces or pressures deeply rooted in each individual and between the individual and his/her environment. (One should not forget that the presence or absence of other individuals is an element in the environment of any particular individual.) The emotional system of the individual is identical to instinct. It forms the internal guidance system of the organism. All animate life has some sort of guiding system. In simple living things a chemical or electrical system serves this function. In more complex life forms a central nervous system serves to coordinate various other systems.

The most obvious manifestation of the emotional system is the reactivity of the individual to its environment. It seems likely that reactivity is rooted in physiology, in the cells and organ systems of the body and not just in the brain. The tight stomach, sweating palms, pounding heart, and various other individually characteristic physiological signs of arousal often precede the awareness of a feeling of anxiety. With sufficient intensity of arousal the organism acts automatically in a characteristic pattern of behavior. Such reflexive behavior impacts upon other individuals, who react in turn. The result is a pattern of behavior for the group or unit as a whole.

Examples of reactivity range from the subtle to the overt. A mother automatically begins to scan her surroundings upon hearing her child's distress cry, even if she has been absorbed in conversation or some other form of activity. A father automatically brushes away the hand of another adult male as he moves closer to examine an insect the second male has noticed in the hair of the father's infant son. A son cringes involuntarily as he hears a certain tone in his father's voice directed in anger toward a sibling. A speaker begins to perspire as she hears her introduction to the podium. These are but a few simple examples.

The level of reactivity of an individual and of a group is believed to be the product of several factors. The internal guidance system of any organism and any species is the result of millions of years of evolutionary development. It is the outcome of the endless struggles of countless individuals within a species to survive and to mate. More immediately it is the product of the experiences of recent generations in the organism's immediate line of descent, in human terms the extended family. Finally the history of the organism or group of organisms interacting with one another in the immediate past plays a role.

Bowen observed that people vary greatly in their ability to manage reactivity. As anxiety increases, so does the tendency to react emotionally and to lose sight of a broader, more objective picture. Some people appear to function with continued emotional reactivity. Life for them is primarily a matter of feeling good or feeling poorly. Slight surges of anxiety appear to produce intensely reactive postures. Such individuals are generally either highly involved with important others or withdrawn. Life's troubles affect people with this level of automatic emotional response frequently and severely.

On the other hand there are people who appear to have greater control of their reactive responses. While they react emotionally at times, their major life decisions appear to be based more on careful thought and clearly defined principles than on reactivity. They can enter into intimate relationships with other people and not have life governed solely by those relationships. They do not deny, however, the importance of relationship. Such people have a degree of choice. They can respond to a situation emotionally or in a less emotional, more thoughtful manner. And they have less reactivity to anxiety in other people.

The concept of differentiation eliminates the need for a concept of normalcy. Any level on the continuum is both natural and normal. Nor is any level particularly concerned with pathology. People and families at any point on the scale can appear to function very well with little overt difficulty. As long as a family can maintain a tolerable level of emotional equilibrium, it can function very well indeed. However the level of differentiation of a family or an individual plays an important role in the family's ability to adapt to changing conditions. Said slightly differently, the level of differentiation plays a role in the ability of the family to absorb and manage tension produced by changing conditions.

The term *differentiation* is borrowed from biology and suggests an analogy to cellular development. From essentially the same material cells develop, or differentiate, to perform separate yet related functions in the organism. The comparison with the development of the individual in the family is illlustrative of the goal of remaining in viable emotional contact with the family yet retaining the ability to function with responsible autonomy.

The basic level of differentiation of self is manifested in the degree to which an individual manages across life to keep thinking and emotional systems separate, to retain choice between behavior governed by thinking and by emotional reactivity, and to set a life course based on carefully thought out principles and goals. The basic level of differentiation of self for any person is believed to develop and become fixed early in life. For a particular individual, the level is generally similar to that of his or her parents. In a group of siblings, one child may be a little more differentiated than the parents and another a little less. The basis for this difference will be addressed in a later discussion of the multigenerational transmission process.

The distinction between thinking and emotional reactivity can be elusive. Many emotional processes involve mental activity. For example, paranoia, fantasies and acts of revenge, panic and anxiety, and the many manifestations of love involve a kind of thinking. Such processes are characterized by a narrow perspective, an overassessment of the importance of self, and the tendency to place the locus of a problem outside of self. Dichotomies or a kind of either-or statement of a problem tend simplistically to reduce inherent complexity and many-sidedness. Often such mental processes are acutely attuned to the real or imagined impact of another on oneself. One is aware where the other is "unfair," "stupid," and so on, in a manner that impinges upon oneself. Such fantasies, often quite accurate within a narrow viewpoint, form the basis for an effort to make the other different. At the same time he or she is highly sensitive to the other, the individual is rarely aware of his or her effect on the other.

In contrast a kind of clear thought is also available to the human at least some of the time. Marked by a broad perspective, such clear thought incorporates complexity and avoids simplistic efforts to fix blame or causality. Such clear thought allows the individual to be more aware of the impact of self on another. Principles or beliefs, anchored in careful thought, can be worked out to maintain one's heading on a life course.

One could also present the distinction between thinking and emotional reactivity in terms of objectivity and subjectivity. The very nature of the brain as an internal organ rules out any complete objectivity. Nonetheless it is possible to distinguish between a narrowly subjective focus and a broader, more objective perspective. The former defines self as the center of the universe and the measure of all that occurs. The latter maintains a wider view of self as a responding, at times inconsequential part of a larger world.

While the basic level of differentiation is established early in life, it can be expanded in later life through a disciplined effort. This is the heart of Family Systems Therapy. A person's level of differentiation can best be observed in an anxious family setting. To the degree that one can thoughtfully guide personal behavior in accordance with well-defined principles in spite of intense anxiety in the family, he or she displays a level or degree of differentiation.

The basic level of differentiation is solid and impervious to relationship variables. In contrast, the functional level of differentiation refers to shifts within the emotional system. Fluctuation in the anxiety level the person experiences determines the functional level of differentiation. When calm, a person may function with a thoughtful approach to life. In the crucible of an intense personal relationship, however, calm thought and self-direction are eroded and life course comes to conform with the demands of the relationship.

The functional level of differentiation can improve or deteriorate in response to relationship variables. An individual with poor functioning may show dramatic improvement following a divorce. Similarly a person who has been functioning well may become dysfunctional when entering or renewing an intense relationship. Such shifts do not represent a change in the basic level of differentiation but reflect the waxing and waning of personal anxiety and the mechanisms that absorb it. The next concept, the triangle, will focus more on this process.

THE TRIANGLE

A two-person relationship behaves in predictable and automatic ways when anxiety resides in either or both partners. The concept of the triangle describes that automatic, predictable behavior. The term *triangle*, used originally by Bowen to describe that phenomenon, has become a of the family-therapy field.

The operation of the triangle is so automatic in daily life that people are generally unaware of their involvement in it. Essentially a two-person relationship is unstable when tense or anxious. Often the discomfort of anxiety will reside more in one than the other of the pair. When anxiety exceeds a tolerable level in the individual, he or she automatically moves to involve a significant third person. This movement generally occurs with an effort to talk with a third person about the stressful relationship and the other partner.

The triangle occurs continually in the daily interaction of people. When the situation is relatively calm, the movement is so subtle and natural that observation is difficult. The triangle is best seen in a moderate degree of stress. At that point the pattern unfolds clearly yet does not tend to spill over into other interlocking relationships, which occurs when anxiety is high. When anxiety is great, the basic triangle can no longer contain and dissolve the tension, which spreads through the web of interlocking triangles.

The effect of involving a third person in a tense two-person relationship initially is often calming. The contact with the outsider tends to decrease the arousal of the anxious partner. The original partner may note the change with relief. His or her troubled partner is no longer so difficult. The relationship between the third person and the original partner, however, may become more tense in the process. An important variable is the intensity of the new relationship between the outsider and the less comfortable half of the original twosome. The more intense that relationship, the more likely the original partner will react to the other's new involvement.

A clear example of the triangle exists in the affair. It is not uncommon to find one spouse involved in an affair of mild to moderate intensity, which appears to have a calming effect on the marriage. Often the other spouse will not be aware of the partner's involvement. Should that same affair, however, become more intense, the uninvolved spouse becomes aware of it quickly and often reacts strongly. How the other spouse learns of the affair is not clear. It often appears to happen accidentally, yet such accidental discoveries follow closely upon the heels of an increase of emotional involvement in the affair.

In a characteristic triangle there are two relatively calm relationships and one anxious relationship. The intense relationship may shift around the three sides of the triangle, or it may become fixed in a particular relationship. When free of anxiety, the participants in the triangle may appear relatively autonomous and free from intense involvement with one another. As anxiety increases, however, the patterns emerge in their predictable fashion.

Another example may help illustrate the process. The involvement of father, mother, and child may take the following form. When anxious, the mother may become more worried about and focused upon her child. In response the child may behave in a way that increases the mother's anxiety. As her discomfort mounts, the mother turns toward the father with her complaints and worries about the child. This movement temporarily relieves her discomfort, but increases that of the father. If he attempts to intervene with the child, the tension is likely to shift from the relationship between the mother and child to that between the father and the child. At that point the relationship between father and mother and mother and child are relatively calm. If he attempts to intervene with the child to enforce discipline or in some other manner straighten out the child, the latter may complain to or in some other fashion reinvolve the mother on its behalf. At that point the tension becomes localized between the parents, leaving the child relatively free of the anxiety. The discomfort of marital tension, however, may rekindle the level of anxiety in the mother, which triggers her worry and focus on the child. In this manner the tension has come full circle to where it began.

In many families the pattern of the central triangle is fluid as illustrated in this example. In other families it may have a chronic regularity. The tension may always remain fixed between the mother and the child with the father in a remote, detached position. Or the tension may be located chronically between the marital partners with the child in the outside position and available for brief episodes of involvement.

When circumstances are calm, the comfortable and desirable position for an individual is to be a part of the twosome. In these circumstances the outsider is seeking to enter the warmth and positive intensity of a twosome. When the situation is anxiety producing, however, the outside, uninvolved position is the desirable one. In this manner the dance of life continues. The greater the degree of undifferentiation in the individuals and the family and the more intense the anxiety, the more active and influential triangles become.

The system of interlocking triangles that comes into play when anxiety can no longer be contained within a single triangle is identifiable with a high degree of accuracy within a given family. When the forces within a particular triangle cannot be shifted, one of the involved twosome will bring in a fourth person. The original third is only temporarily discarded and can be reinvolved at a later time. In this manner various important persons become involved, both from inside and outside the family. Depending upon the level of anxiety in the family, various additional triangles are stirred up and return to dormancy in a predictable fashion.

In summary, the concept of the triangle addresses the automatic movement of individuals to maintain the degree of involvement or noninvolvement with another that allows them the greatest freedom from anxiety. It also addresses the mechanisms involved in anxiety transfer and arousal of the broader family group.

NUCLEAR FAMILY EMOTIONAL PROCESS

Each partner comes to a marriage with a specific level of autonomous self or differentiation and a level of emotional connectedness or undifferentiation. Bowen Theory suggests that marital partners have similar levels of differentiation and undifferentiation. In the closeness of an intense relationship the emotional selves of each blend or fuse together into a common self, a "we-ness." Each partner attempts to deal with the intensity of this common self by using mechanisms similar to those he or she used in relationship to the parents. The outcome of these efforts to survive the intensity of the relationship are a set of four mechanisms or patterns that operate in the nuclear family (parents and children). Families may display a mixture of all four mechanisms. Less frequently the intensity will propel a single mechanism that tends to be an extreme example of a type of family interaction.

The greater the level of fusion or "we-ness" of the marital pair, the greater the likelihood that these mechanisms will be used frequently. A second important variable is the level of anxiety in the family at any point in time. Where a family lives with a chronic level of anxiety, one or more of the mechanisms are at work continuously. Changes in the intensity or frequency of the pattern will then occur in response to acute anxiety. A family with a lower level of chronic anxiety may reveal its mechanisms only in the presence of acute anxiety.

These mechanisms, generally played out in the marital relationship, are always able to trigger the triangle described previously. The outsider, however, is not necessarily a child. This has theoretical importance in that mechanisms between the parents do not necessarily impair the functioning of children. For example, a child may develop relatively well in spite of a conflictual relationship between the parents. The four patterns or mechanisms of nuclear family emotional process are emotional distance, marital conflict, dysfunction in a spouse, and transmission of the the problem to a child.

Emotional Distance

Many people react to the intensity of emotional contact by pulling away. The effects of such involvement with the other are so uncomfortable that people draw back as if from a hot stove. Often the emotionality is negatively charged, although too much positive togetherness can also produce this emotional reflex.

The distance can be actual or it can be the result of a series of internal operations that effectively shield a person from contact with another. Where the distance is external, one spouse may find a way to spend much time away from the other. For example he or she may seek employment requiring a great deal of travel. Long work hours coupled with heavy community involvement may achieve the same result. The outcome is that the marital pair actually spend very little time together. When they are together it may be in the company of other people at meetings or social events. In effect the opportunities for intense contact are greatly reduced or avoided.

While equally effective at reducing emotional contact, the internal processes to attain distance are often more subtle and difficult to spot. Chronic irritability, involvement in a book or activity to the exclusion of all else, a stony or troubled countenance, and the ability to tune out the efforts of the other to communicate all may manifest an internal shutting down of emotional repsonse. At the same time that one is closing off contact, thoughts of the other may fill thinking time.

A further example may provide greater clarity of the process. A family seen in clinical practice reported that, over the years, they gradually came to speak less and less to one another. The husband reported that he had never been able to get his wife to see anything his way, and she in turn reported that he never seemed to understand her. Both came to believe it was simply easier not to try to engage the other. Each complained of loneliness. The wife complained that the spouse spent much of his time with a book or in front of the television set. The husband responded that the wife spent much of her time on the phone to other people. Yet while each avoided contact with the other, their fantasies and thoughts were often directed toward the other in a critical manner.

Distancing occurs automatically and generally without the partners being acutely aware of it. Over time it comes to be an accepted way of living so long as nothing exacerbates the level of anxiety the mechanism diffuses. It is, in effect, a safety valve built into the relationship to "bleed off" tension. One partner may be aware of the distance and make efforts to engage the other. Generally this is futile and becomes a stimulus to greater distance in the other. If a partner persists in attempting to engage the other, the pattern may shift to one of marital conflict followed by periods of distance. Yet when anxiety is reduced, this same pair may be able to communicate about all sorts of things and actually seek out one another.

Although distancing is automatic, it usually produces more distance than people want. If the discomfort of the distance becomes great enough in one, the involvement of a significant other in a triangle occurs. What people are actually avoiding is their own discomfort or reactivity to another. Characteristically however, they tend to view the other, rather than their own reactivity, as the cause of their discomfort (Kerr, 1981).

Marital Conflict

Marital conflict is widely acknowledged as a symptom of tension in a family. Its function as a mechanism to manage anxiety and maintain a degree of equilibrium in the family is less readily recognized. It exists, as do all such mechanisms, on a continuum from mild to severe. Critical variables are the degree of fusion of the marital pair and the level or intensity of the anxiety that propels the process.

In the moderately to highly anxious variants of marital conflict, partners have high emotional reactivity to one another. Often the thoughts of one or both are focused on the "obstinate, uncaring, unreasonable" qualities of the other. In such situations conflict can flare with apparently little provocation and quickly escalate in intensity. It is not uncommon for years-old grievances to be brought forth yet again. The effect is usually similar to pouring gasoline on smoldering coals. If the intensity of the conflict exceeds the capacity of the relationship to manage it, the automatic movement to bring in a significant third occurs. In extreme examples, outside agencies intervene in the form of the police and various crisis intervention services.

The cycle of marital conflict and ensuing distance is a familiar one. Often the conflictual episodes are followed by an equally intense period of warm togetherness. As the inevitable tension builds once again, closeness gives way to distance and ultimately conflict. During the quiet but distanced phases, one or both partners may be reviewing their arguments and monitoring the other for continued evidence of fault. These revised arguments and new "facts" become further ammunition in subsequent conflict.

In marital conflict it is characteristic for such partners to be heavily focused upon one another. The partner's flaws are noted in great detail and often accurately. At the same time, neither really understands the role of self in the pattern. People sometimes preface an attack on the other with a comment like "I know I have a role in this, but ...." What they seem to mean is that whatever minor role they have played, it has been in the nature of self-defense and is simply inconsequential when compared to the "atrocities" of the other. The inability to gain any objective view of self in the pattern makes it difficult to master one's own emotional reactivity in the situation.

There is often concern about children raised in a family with intense marital conflict. This is a difficult area, and the assumption is often made that marital conflict inevitably harms the child. Yet from a theoretical perspective, the more anxiety can be contained and managed in the marital unit, the less likely it is to effect the child's development. Again important variables are the degree of fusion in the family and the intensity of anxiety.

Clinical observation suggests that children run a greater risk when the parent becomes anxious about the effects of marital interaction upon the child. That anxiety shapes the parent's interaction with the child and can involve the child in the emotional process of the marriage. For example, concerned about a child's reaction to heated exchanges in the marital unit, a parent may attempt to compensate by becoming overly optimistic or feigning light-heartedness in the presence of the child. The child may respond by sensing the parent's mood and also becoming overly positive or overly negative. The child may also react to the parent's concern by pushing limits. Or the child may attempt to support the parent, in effect taking sides in the marital conflict. Such anxious involvement of a parent with a child is the basis for the third major mechanism of nuclear family emotional process.

Transmission of the Problem to a Child

All children become involved to a degree in the emotional process of the parents. This is the basis of a concept of Family Systems Theory to be discussed later, the Multigenerational Transmission Process. In some families, however, the process is so intense or major that it stands out clearly and results in the impairment of the child's ability to function in life. This process is believed to play a part in schizophrenia and other severe and difficult symptoms.

In simplistic terms, anxiety in a parent is expressed in sensitivity and reactivity to a child. The parent directly involved is the primary caretaker, generally the mother, but the other parent's position and ability to relate to the primary caretaker is an integral part of the process. To isolate the phenomenon in a particular generation of parent and child is somewhat misleading. That framework too easily allows the assignment of blame to the parent and the status of victim to the child. Such a viewpoint misses completely the long-range sweep of the phenomenon across the generations of a family. It also seriously misgauges the automatic, even physiological proportions of the relationship between parent and child and parent to parent. In intense versions the union approaches symbiosis in the biological sense of the word. Each person appears to have lost the ability to function and even to survive independently in the world.

The process is relatively easy to describe. It is far more difficult to explain. The mother's emotional response to the child affects her ability to mother competently. The involvement may appear as a positive, loving involvement or as nagging worry. In the former the mother characteristically has difficulty setting appropriate limits to the child's behavior. Nothing is too good for her child, who can also do no wrong. In the worrisome version the mother focuses on a real or supposed problem in the child. The presumed problem can be physical or psychological. She appears both to want the child to be independent yet afraid to let him or her move beyond the range of her guidance and control. The child also behaves as if it cannot function without such guidance. He or she may be fearful or new situations or overly bold.

It is unclear how the mother and child become sensitized and linked emotionally. It may occur prior to birth in the physiological interaction of mother and fetus. Perhaps it occurs in the earliest mother-child interaction following birth. It may be a gradually evolving process over time with each anxious exchange furthering the process, or it may be all of the above. The child plays a role in the process. He or she behaves in a manner that will justify the mother's concern. Simple random chance may play a role. Unexpected illness in the child or the parent during a formative period may accelerate the union. Or it may simply be a necessary process that gets out of hand due to the chance removal of as yet unknown inhibitory or repressor mechanisms.

The father's role is as important as the mother's in the process, although she may be the parent most directly involved with the child. Anxiety in the relationship between the parents directly relates to the involvement of the child. The father's lack of differentiation in the relationship directly impacts upon the mother's ability to view herself and her child objectively. There are many versions of paternal behavior in the process. He may be aware of the mother's difficulty being objective about her child. He may see the child as weak or spoiled and in some fashion try to compensate. He may be overly harsh or become involved in efforts to strengthen or toughen the child. The effect is to push the mother and child closer together. The mother may approach the the father with her concerns. He may support her concern and assist by seeking or encouraging professional help. If he responds with criticism or distance, he tends to increase the mother's anxiety, driving the process even further. Heightened emotionality between the parents tends to result in greater maternal involvement with the child.

It is important to note that this process is driven by anxiety in the parent at least initially. The child in this position develops a heightened sensitivity to emotional forces in the family and particularly to anxiety in the mother. Although in the early stages the anxiety is located in the parent, the process eventually can be activated by anxiety in either mother, father, or child.

Dysfunction in a Spouse

The fourth pattern or mechanism of nuclear family emotional process concerns the adaptivity of spouses to one another. In most marriages there are continual compromises in which one spouse yields to the other to avoid conflict. This pattern is highly functional and is effective to a point in containing anxiety and preserving harmony. In many marriages the adaptivity is two-sided with each yielding in one situation or another.

In some marriages, however, the pattern can become intense and fixed. The outcome is decreased functioning in one and an apparent overfunctioning of the other. In an early paper (1959) Bowen described the pattern in the following manner. "One denies the immaturity and functions with a facade of adequacy. The other accentuates the immaturity and functions with a facade of inadequacy. Neither can function in the midground between over-adequacy and inadequacy" (Bowen, 1959, p. 19). In a sense, this arrangement is functional. Without someone taking charge, such families might never be able to reach decisions. The price is high, however.

The pressures toward this outcome can come from both partners. The overfunctioning spouse may have been trained to decide for others in the family he or she came from. The underfunctioning one may have been accustomed to let other people make decisions for self. Generally the overfunctioning one appears strong and capable. Occasionally the underfunctioning one may look great, while the supporting mate is a wreck. In this case the efforts of one to prop up and support the other have been successful. The supported one makes the decisions that the other has to live with and implement. As in most areas of family functioning, the pattern is clear, but precisely how it happens is not.

An example may help to describe the process. Mr. and Mrs. K were seen upon referral from the medical service of a general hospital. Mrs. K reported that her husband had seemed increasingly withdrawn and did little to care for himself. Mrs. K was the oldest of several children. At a young age she had begun to look after her siblings as her mother struggled to meet the family bills. Mr. K was the youngest son of several siblings. He was his mother's favorite and had married late. Mrs. K had handled most of the family's activities, including raising their two children. Mr. K functioned moderately well at his employment, but was very content to allow Mrs. K to handle most matters at home. Over the years she also took on the management of her aging mother's affairs and became highly competent in her career. Mrs. K reported that she had noted that Mr. K did less and less as time went on.

About ten years prior to their referral, several important family members had been unexpectedly killed in an accident. Mrs. K reported that she had picked up the reins and helped everyone through the crisis. She said she knew she had to do it. She continued to be involved in aiding the survivors to manage their lives. From the point of the accident, Mr. K's functioning declined more rapidly. Mrs. K took over managing Mr. K's health management. She arranged his medical consultations, made sure he followed the doctor's orders, and tried to interpret his condition to the medical staff. As his functioning deteriorated, she maintained his personal hygiene and supervised all his activities. As his condition worsened, Mrs. K reported that he was pleasant to everyone else but would become very angry and rebellious with her. These episodes occurred at times when she had been more active than usual trying to help him and keep him on course. Eventually Mr. K received a diagnosis of Alzheimer's disease and was placed in a care facility. At that point Mrs. K's health rapidly deteriorated.

When anxiety is low, the dysfunction may not be evident. Under conditions of sustained chronic anxiety, the low functioning individual may develop a physical, emotional, or social dysfunction. The course of the dysfunction may ebb and flow in response to levels of anxiety. The pressure of the symptom across time, however, can result in new roles or postures for family members that actually work to decrease relationship tension in the family (Kerr, 1981). Nursing and caretaker roles around the dysfunctional person can ease interpersonal tension. It is as if some gain identity and purpose at the expense of another.

FAMILY PROJECTION PROCESS

The concept describes the basic process by which parental problems can be projected onto a child or children. It concerns a mother's emotional sensitivity to a child that is greater than that to her spouse. The husband is sensitive to his wife's anxiety and supports her involvement with the child or children.

In a family the mother's level of emotional involvement varies among the children. Characteristically her sensitivity and response is greater to one child than to the others. Anxiety heightens her feeling for the child. She responds as if the anxiety were in the child rather than in her. The involvement usually begins at birth. The mother's feelings can be intense and range from an overpositive, protective posture to revulsion. The child becomes sensitive to the anxiety in the mother. The father either supports her emotional involvement with the child or withdraws from it.

The dysfunction of the parents as a unit leads to the inclusion of the child in the emotional process between them. Where other mechanisms of anxiety management are effective for the parents, the involvement of the child may occur only occasionally with little or no observable impairment of the child. Any set of parents, however, is merely the current embodiment of forces or processes that have been active for many generations before them. Each parent has been involved to some degree in the emotional configuration of his or her own parents, and those parents with their parents, and so on back in time.

The process is marked initially by emotional shifts within the parental unit that are expressed in the mother's response to the child. If positive, she may overvalue, overprotect, and in general behave in ways that foster immaturity in the child. If negative, she may be overly harsh and restrictive. It is important to remember that the process appears to originate in the parent. The child quickly comes to play a role, however, with behavior that triggers the mother's anxiety and attention. Sometimes the process involves only one child, and other siblings remain relatively free from involvement. If the anxiety is intense enough, however, it may "spill over" to involve other siblings to a greater degree. The functioning of such compromised children is labile, tending to improve or decline in response to anxiety in relationships of importance to them. It is this basic process that appears to underlie schizophrenia.

While the attachment is generally most observable between mother and child, the father is equally involved in the process. The level of his own anxiety and the mechanisms he employs to preserve his own functioning have great impact on the mother and the child. If he withdraws, the intensity between mother and child is increased. If he supports her concern the problem tends to become more firmly fixed in the child. There are some families where the projection process appears to operate through the father rather than the mother. This appears to occur where the mother is absent or in some other fashion unavailable.

Neither parent nor child is at fault in this process. Neither father nor mother wants this sort of emotional involvement with the child. The parents may have some awareness of the intensity of the relationships but find themselves unable to be different. Such interlocking sensitivity and reactivity between mother and child can be seen in other life-forms. Jane Goodall reports on the relationship between a chimpanzee mother, Flo, and her son Flint (Goodall, 1979). Although Flo appeared to be an excellent mother and had produced older children who became dominant animals in the chimpanzee community, her relationship to Flint was different. They were unable to accomplish weaning, with Flint clinging to his mother well past the usual age when young males join their adolescent peers. When Flo died in Flint's eighth year, Flint survived her by three and a half weeks.

Similar observations suggest that such a process between mother and child has less to do with human psychology than it does with basic life processes the human has in common with other life-forms. It does not represent the product of a single generation. The intensity of the parent-child involvement is characteristic of past generations as well. Its appearance and intensity in one generation is the cumulative effect of what has happened in preceding generations. This is the basis for the fifth concept of Bowen Theory.

THE MULTIGENERATIONAL TRANSMISSION PROCESS

The family projection process operates generation after generation in a family. It is noticeable only when it is moderately intense. In milder varieties it is so common a process that people regard it simply as a part of living and a natural union between parent and child. As noted previously, the mechanism has more to do with parental sensitivity and than with the actual needs of the child.

In a group of siblings one child is more involved in the process than the others, although if intense enough other siblings can be involved. The invested child develops a heightened sensitivity to emotion in the parents, who react in the manner described previously. Other brothers and sisters tend to be less sensitive to parental emotion.

They grow up with a greater degree of separation between thinking and feeling. They are somewhat more differentiated than their more compromised sibling. They tend to learn more from the parents' strengths. The involved child learns about and stimulates the parents' emotional immaturity.

The invested or focused child is believed to have a slightly lower level of differentiation than that of the parents. The less involved children develop similar or slightly higher levels of differentiation than that of the parents. This variation has important theoretical implications for life course. People with somewhat higher levels of differentiation are better able to set a thoughtful and more objective life course. They are less vulnerable to the consequences of prolonged emotional intensity.

Bowen Theory suggests that people marry partners with a level of differentiation similar to their own. Over the generations, therefore, the invested children of each generation marry partners and operate with greater emotional intensity than did their parents. Their siblings create families with emotional levels that are similar to or less intense than those of the original family. From this perspective in any family there are lines moving through time toward greater and lesser levels of differentiation. The end point of such a progression towards undifferentiation is thought to be the intense varieties of dysfunction. Forms of schizophrenia, chronic alcoholism, and possibly even chronic physical illness are believed to be manifestations of highly intense versions of this process.

In any particular generation fortuitous events can slow the process down. Similarly, unfavorable circumstances can speed it up. The ability of mechanisms other than the projection process to absorb anxiety in a marriage is an important variable. On some level change in society and subsequent fluctuations in anxiety can play a role. Disappearance of needed resources and overpopulation appear to be major contributors to societal anxiety.

Precisely how the mother-child involvement develops is not clear. Oldest or youngest children appear to be involved frequently with the mother. The only child of a given sex among the siblings, for example the only boy or the only girl, also is a likely candidate. Children born with or who have developed a physical problem are also often involved. Yet many children in such positions do not become the object of parental anxiety, suggesting that other mechanisms or factors effect which children become involved in the process.

SIBLING POSITION

In 1961, Walter Toman published *Family Constellation: A Psychological Game*. Based on the collection of data from several hundred families, Toman's work presented profiles of the characteristics of people who occupy any of ten sibling positions. While these descriptions are not meant to be precise for a particular person, they indicate trends and patterns of behavior that generally characterize persons occupying a given sibling position.

According to Toman, marriage partners have complementary, partially complementary, or noncomplementary sibling positions. The level or degree of complementarity depends upon the presence or absence of rank and/or sex conflict. For example, two oldest children or two youngest children would have a rank conflict. While each could identify with the other, each would tend to seek the same role. The expectations and behavior of one would not complement the other. A brother of brothers or a sister of sisters would have a sex conflict. Neither would have had the experience of a sibling of the opposite sex. Partially complementary relationships involve partners with middle sibling positions. Each spouse would have at least one sibling relationship that would complement at least one sibling relationship of the other. Partners with noncomplementary sibling positions would present either or both a rank and sex conflict. Toman suggests marital partners with noncomplementary sibling positions have greater difficulty in marriage than partners with complementary or partially complementary relationships.

Degrees of complementarity can also be applied to parent-child relationships. Parents and offspring with rank and/or sex conflict could be expected to have greater difficulty adjusting to one another than those who do not. The interactional expectations of the parent would not fit the behavior of the child. Whatever the degree of complementarity, however, each person comes to a marriage with a series of expectations and reactive types of behavior that are determined by one's own sibling position.

Toman's work clarified and organized much of Bowen's thinking along similar lines. Toman studied normal families, and the work does not take into consideration the effects of the family projection process. The anxious focus of this process can blur and erode the characteristics of the person's sibling position, no matter where in the birth order it falls. Nevertheless, Toman's profiles provide a way to acquire presumptive knowledge about the nature of relationships by knowing only the sibling position of each partner. Each departure from what might be expected provides another piece of information about the operation of emotional forces in the family. The profiles also permit the reconstruction of presumable relationship patterns in past generations, making it possible to trace the evolving pattern of family interaction backwards in time.

Anxiety plays a role in the expression of sibling position characteristics in a family. An anxious older brother of brothers can become more dogmatic and authoritarian than is the case when he is calmer. The youngest sister of several brothers may appear more "helpless" and needy when anxious than when not. In clinical practice, the knowledge of sibling position characteristics may provide a person a first glimpse of his or her own reactive behavior and its impact on another.

EMOTIONAL CUTOFF

The concept of emotional cutoff addresses the manner in which people attempt to manage the emotional attachment to their parents and important other individuals. One may resort to intrapsychic means to deny the attachment, or one may actually separate oneself physically from the family and reduce contact to infrequent, highly controlled interactions. Some mix of these mechanisms may also be employed.

By the use of intrapsychic mechanisms to manage the discomfort of attachment, a person can remain in frequent contact with important others and even live under the same roof. Yet he or she remains insulated or out of contact with the parents. At the extreme of this mechanism is the adult child who lives in isolation in the parental home. Psychosis in such an individual may represent an exaggerated version of this process. Bowen notes that the person who uses such internal mechanisms to manage attachment maintains some level of supportive contact to the parents and is more likely to develop internalized symptoms like physical illness or depression (Bowen, 1976).

At the other end of the continuum is the person who uses physical distance to achieve the same outcome, that is management of unresolved attachment to the parents and important others. The distance may be punctuated with regular "duty visits," or it may be marked by the avoidance of all contact. Duty visits tend to be characterized by a certain pattern or ritual that minimizes person-to-person contact. Often the cutoff individual blames the parents for the distance and misses the role that he or she plays in the process.

The emotional cutoff is a natural process. On a simple level people speak of the need for personal space or sometimes even freedom as a means of "explaining" their avoidance of others. Distance seems to be the safety valve of the emotional system. Yet at the same time distance leaves people primed for closeness. In extreme examples people constantly search for closeness but react intensely to it when they stumble over it. This phenomenon may play a role in the often heard lament "We love each other but we just can't seem to live together." The more an individual employs cutoff to manage attachment to parents and the original family, the greater his or her vulnerability to intense emotional processes in current relationships.

Although the cutoff appears to handle the relationship to parents, the individual remains vulnerable to other intense relationships. He or she has not found a way to relate to another but has merely removed oneself from the emotional presence of the other. In marriage frequently a pattern and level of intensity can develop that is similar to that from which one cut off in the original family. The pattern of cutoff is carried over into other intense relationships. In extreme outcomes the person may go from relationship to relationship, seeking the positive effects of closeness yet automatically cutting off when the intensity reaches a certain tolerance level. In another variation, the individual may give up on relationships altogether, maintaining a relatively fixed distance from all others.

EMOTIONAL PROCESSES IN SOCIETY

The eighth concept in the Bowen Family Systems Theory extends thinking to emotional processes operating in society. Essentially these processes are similar to those of the family and reflect the operation of the togetherness force and the individuation force. As in the family, the critical factor is the intensity of anxiety in society at a given point in time. The greater the level of anxiety, the more intensely the movement toward togetherness erodes individuation. Bowen (1978, p. 272) postulates that "man's increasing anxiety is a product of population explosion, the disappearance of new habitable land to colonize, the approaching depletion of raw materials necessary to sustain life, and growing awareness that 'spaceship earth' cannot indefinitely support human life in the style to which man and his technology have become accustomed."

Bowen became interested in the way anxious parents deal with teenage behavior problems and the way society through its represen-tatives deals with the same phenomenon. Anxious public officials, like anxious parents, lose sight of beliefs and principles when dealing with their problem children. Their decisions reflect efforts to relieve anxious discomfort rather than adherence to carefully established guidelines.

A teenager's anxious demand for "rights" can shatter a poorly constructed system of belief in a parent. Without clear principles to guide their decisions, parents tend either to yield to the child in an effort to appease, or display reactive rigidity and harshness not merited by the situation. As the child exploits the insecurity of the parents, they respond with an intensified focus on the child and demands that he or she must change. The cycle of acting out and appeasement or repression can escalate quickly. Public officials do little better than the parents in managing the anxiety generated in the effort to deal with the out-of-control teenager.

Bowen's observations have led him to believe that the functional level of differentiation in society has decreased in the past twenty-five years (Bowen, 1978). Increasing population and dwindling resources produce anxiety that drives societal regression, as Bowen originally described the process. New frontiers are disappearing, and it is difficult to distance from spreading population density. Heightened anxiety in society produces a surge of togetherness, which in turn creates greater discomfort and further anxiety.

In an anxious social climate, the societal projection process has intensified (Bowen, 1978). In this process two people or groups join together and enhance their own fucntioning at the expense of a third party. The greater the level of anxiety in society, the more this mechanism becomes active as a way of binding or absorbing that anxiety. This is similar to what happens in the family projection process. The twosome can force the third into submission, the outsider can force the other two to treat him or her as impaired, or the projection can fit together like a tongue and groove with each side matching the expectation of the other. Each position is functional in the system; that is, each plays a specific role in the management of anxiety. It is not possible to reduce the intensity of the projection process without first reducing the emotionality that propels it.

The emotional climate and processes of society represent yet another element in the emotional climate of the family. The anxious society, like the anxious family, has difficulty resolving its problems without polarization around an issue, cutoff, reciprocal over- and underfunctioning, and so forth. The result is a series of crises, generally resolved on the basis of restoring comfort rather than a thoughtful approach based upon principles and a degree of respect for differing viewpoints.

References

Bowen, M. (1959). Family relationship in schizophrenia. In A. Auerbach (Ed.), *Schizophrenia: An integrated approach* (pp. 147-178). New York: Ronald Press.

Bowen M. (1961). Family psychotherapy. *American Journal of Orthopsychiatry, 1*(1), 40-60.

Bowen, M. (1966). The use of theory in clinical practice. *Comprehensive Psychiatry, 7*, 345-374.

Bowen, M. (1971). Family therapy and family group therapy. In H. Kaplan & B. Saddock (Eds.), *Comprehensive group psychotherapy* (pp. 384-421). Baltimore: Williams and Wilkins.

Bowen, M. (1976). Theory in the practice of psychotherapy. In P. Guerin (Ed.), *Family therapy*. New York: Gardner Press.

Bowen, M. (1978). Societal regression as viewed through family systems theory. In M. Bowen (Ed.), *Family therapy in clinical practice* (pp. 269-282). New York: Jason Aronson.

Bowen, M., Dysinger, R. H., & Basmania, B. (1959). The role of the father in families with a schizophrenic patient. *American Journal of Psychiatry, 115*, 1017-1020.

Bowen, M., Dysinger, R. H., Brady, W. M., & Basmania, B. (1978). Treatment of family groups with a schizophrenic member. In M. Bowen (Ed.), *Family therapy in clinical practice* (pp. 3-15). New York: Jason Aronson.

Goodall, J. (1979). Warfare and cannibalism among Gombe's chimpanzees. *National Geographic, 155*(5) 593-621.

Kerr, M. E. (1981). Family systems theory and therapy. In A. Gurman & P. Kniskern (Eds.), *Handbook of family therapy* (pp. 226-264). New York: Knopf.

Toman, W. (1961). *Family constellation: A psychological game*. New York: Springer.

Chapter 4

Family Systems Theory in Clinical Practice

The most important goal or outcome of Family Systems Therapy is improved differentiation of self (Bowen, 1974). The effort toward greater differentiation of self involves recognition of one's sensitivity to others and the automatic or semiautomatic feeling states and behaviors that are associated with such sensitivity. The intensity of one's anxiety and that of the family can affect the effort. Anxiety can be defined simply as fear of a real or imagined threat. On a somewhat different level it can be defined as physiological arousal prepatory to action to preserve the safety of the individual. The greater the level of anxiety, the more behavior becomes automatic or "instinctual."

A second major factor affecting the differentiating effort is the basic level of differentiation of the person. The basic level in anyone is a product of the generations and the parents who raised the individual. Differentiation of self involves the ability of the individual to maintain separation of emotional and intellectual functioning (Bowen, 1976). Emotional functioning refers to the automatic or instinctual responses of the individual to all facets of the environment. Such responses have come collectively to be called reactivity and range from the subtle to the overt. Reactivity is the product of the emotional system, an innate guidance system similar to that which governs instinctual behavior in other life-forms. Intellectual functioning refers to the thinking, reflective capacities of the human. The intellectual or cognitive system of the human has the capacity to observe reactivity and the operation of the emotional system.

The ability to separate emotional and intellectual functioning is relative. When anxiety is sufficiently high, the automatic responses of the emotional system will override cognitive activity. If sufficiently anxious, even the highly differentiated person has difficulty guiding behavior with thought. A person with a lower basic level of differentiation can lose cognitive functioning even at low levels of anxiety.

The effort of Family Systems Therapy is to address the thoughtful capacity of the individual as much as possible. Engagement of the cognitive system can heighten objectivity and broaden perspective. When people begin to become more objective about the situations and the other people to whom they react emotionally, anxiety is automatically lowered. With reduced anxiety, family members become more objective and calmer. Often simply the effort to become more objective relieves anxiety sufficiently that the problem or symptom disappears of its own accord.

Family Systems Therapy begins with a survey of emotional field or system. In essence one wants to know in as clear a fashion as possible how the family functioned across time. In a sense each nuclear family embodies the emotional processes and patterns of the generations that have preceded it. The survey of the family field provides a roadmap or blueprint that the experienced clinician can read and in effect teach to the motivated family.

The information is collected and represented on the family diagram. (The general format is shown in Figure 4.1.) In the diagram males are depicted by squares and the females by circles. The husband and wife of a nuclear family are represented with the male on the left and the female on the right. A solid line connects them. Each of the children they produce is connected to the marital unit by a solid line. The birth order of children is represented by placing the eldest on the left beneath the parents, and each succeeding sibling is placed to the right of the older sibling preceding it. In this manner each successive generation is represented with the most recent generation at the bottom of the diagram.

As each person is added to the diagram, basic information is collected. Vital statistics are important. These include date and place of birth, date, place and cause of death, level of education, brief history of employment, and a survey of major health problems. Dates are important and should be noted for all events listed. Where health problems have been noted, the date of onset, the length and course of treatment, and the outcome should be added to the diagram. In this manner a composite picture of the functioning of each family member is collected.

There are many ways to collect family information. A good way is to simply inquire what has brought people to the point of seeking assistance in the first place. What is the problem, what has been done about it to this point, and how do family members understand what is

FAMILY DIAGRAM

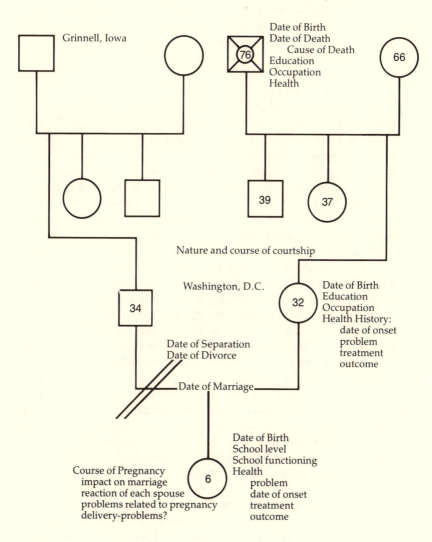

Wellesley, Mass.

Grinnell, Iowa

Date of Birth
Date of Death
    Cause of Death
Education
Occupation
Health

76

66

39   37

Nature and course of courtship

Washington, D.C.

Date of Birth
Education
Occupation
Health History:
    date of onset
    problem
    treatment
    outcome

34   32

Date of Separation
Date of Divorce

Date of Marriage

Date of Birth
School level
School functioning
Health
    problem
    date of onset
    treatment
    outcome

Course of Pregnancy
    impact on marriage
    reaction of each spouse
    problems related to pregnancy
    delivery-problems?

6

Figure 4.1 The Family Diagram

happening in the family are but a few of the early questions that come to mind. Often people will have different points of view about the problem and how it works. In the process of collecting such information, it is relatively easy to gather the vital statistics mentioned above.

Beyond the presenting problem and vital statistics, one begins to collect information about the functioning of the nuclear and extended family systems. The spouses each have a view about the nature and course of their relationship. There have been good times and bad times, periods of tranquility and of great emotional reactivity. Specific dates are always useful. It is important to find out what the difference has been and how each partner explains the change. Changes of employment and of location may have had an impact on family functioning. Part of the chronology of family development includes the dates of such changes and an assessment of how the change has affected the family. Often the thinking of each partner about such changes and moves reveals motivations not at all related to the employment itself. Separations and divorces are important elements in the history of the nuclear family. Each person has a point of view about such events and their effect. Did the separation allow people to function better or did it make things worse? How do people account for the effect? From time to time the composition of the household changes. Children grow up and move away, grandparents come to live with the family, housekeepers come and go. How do such changes appear to have affected the functioning of family members and how do people account for that?

Events and shifts in a nuclear family do not occur in a vacuum. The husband and wife are each a member of extended families whose functioning can affect the nuclear family. Members of the extended family may live nearby or far away. It is important to determine the frequency and nature of the contact with the extended family. How does such contact or its absence affect the nuclear family? Marriages, births, deaths, divorces, and illnesses in the extended family may correspond closely in time to events in the nuclear family. Dates and accurate information as to the nature of events in the extended family are important. In this manner information can be collected on both the vital statistics and the emotional processes of the family across as many generations as possible.

In a sense the family diagram is never completed. There is always more to know. As it develops, basic patterns of emotional reactivity often become clear in the nuclear and extended families. It is possible to determine those who greatly influence the family and those who are more peripheral. Events that have led to major alterations in the functioning of the family become clearer. These are often called *nodal events*. They appear to mark a turning point in the family. For example, the death of an important family member may mark the beginning of a series of problems in a family, a sort of emotional shock wave across the generations. It is important to be able to separate fact from opinion or assumption. Family members have many opinions and assumptions that form the basis for much of their behavior. Yet the web of fact tells a more accurate, sometimes quite different story about the family's development across time.

The squares, circles, and lines of the family diagram are unimportant in themselves. The information of the family diagram is only of use alongside the theoretical thinking of the clinician. It is a part of the overall research orientation of the clinician. In conjunction with theory, the family diagram illuminates nuclear and multigenerational processes and patterns in the family.

The effort of the clinician to maintain a research attitude is important and easily overlooked in efforts to apply Bowen Theory in the clinical setting. The clinician's general posture is one of inquiry. The family diagram provides a roadmap for inquiry. One is interested in the facts of the family. From the facts one can ask dozens of questions about the processes of family functioning. If the questions are truly honest, that is, they represent the goal of acquiring information, they assist the family in its effort to learn more about itself. The clinician does not "do" anything with a particular piece of information. But each bit of fact leads to further inquiry and a clearer view of how each person fits into the patterns and events of the family.

For example, the identification of a nodal event in a family does not provide a particular series of interventions for the clinician. But a range of questions about family functioning become available. How do family members account for the importance of the event? What has assisted or impeded adjustment to the event? Step by step the family and the clinician assist each other with the inquiry. From the information acquired, the therapist can make suggestions or give his or her own opinions. But the effort remains with the family.

The methodology of Family Systems Therapy is relatively simple. It is determined by theoretical considerations as much as possible. To the best of his or her abilities, the clinician attempts to relate calmly and neutrally to the family. He or she does not actively attempt to make the family different. Interventions, or some move or action taken by the therapist to impact upon the family presumably in a positive manner, play little if any role. The clinician focuses on gathering information, maintaining a broad perspective, obtaining and maintaining emotional neutrality, and operating from a research perspective.

Family Systems Therapy does not require the presence of all family members. Often the two spouses are considered the responsible members and seen in therapy. This is not a hard and fast rule however. Various members of the family may be seen at different times reflecting shifts in motivation among family members and the therapist's own efforts to learn more about the family. Theoretical developments in the late 1960s led to an approach that includes only one family member in the session. This process will be discussed later in the chapter.

Bowen (1971) lists four main functions for the therapist with the spouses: (1) defining and clarifying the relationship between the spouses; (2) keeping self detriangled from the family emotional system; (3) teaching the functioning of emotional systems; and (4) demonstrating differentiation by taking "I-positions" during the course of therapy. Each of these functions represents a theoretical perspective and will be discussed in the following paragraphs.

DEFINING AND CLARIFYING THE EMOTIONAL PROCESS BETWEEN SPOUSES

Over the course of a marriage, spouses constantly react emotionally to one another. Each becomes aware of subjects and areas that provoke emotional response in the other. Particularly sensitive areas are dropped from general conversation and interaction. When anxiety is high, one may attack the other on such a "sore point." In effect neither really knows the other. Important thoughts and viewpoints remain hidden. When spouses attempt to talk it out, however, they run a substantial risk of escalating the emotional distance between them. Often the effort to talk occurs when the anxiety in either or both has exceeded tolerable limits. At such times people are more sensitive to one another. They are less able to listen to one another without automatic levels of reactivity. The effort to talk can actually drive people further apart.

The format of therapy aids the therapist in controlling the interchange between spouses. With low-key direct questions and comments the therapist talks to one partner while the other listens. In the initial sessions with an intense pair, it may be difficult for the listening partner not to interrupt and challenge the viewpoint of the other. By becoming more active, the therapist can tone down the reactivity with questions directed to one and the sessions can continue.

When it becomes clear that feelings are being stirred up in a session, the clinician attempts to get people talking about the feelings rather than expressing them. For example, when a husband's voice rises in anger, the therapist may ask the wife if she noted the change in tone and what her thoughts were when she heard it. When such moments threaten to escalate into direct, feeling-laden exchanges between the partners, the therapist can step up the tempo and accentuate the low-keyed, calm nature of his questions. Is the person aware of the triggers that set off the feelings and the reactive response? What is there about self that makes the other so mad? The clinician tries to relate directly to each and to "tone down" an anxious exchange between the spouses. An important general goal is to touch upon emotionally important issues and elicit thoughtful, calm responses (Bowen, 1971).

The questions and comments of the therapist are directed to the thinking rather than the feelings of each spouse. They are designed to tap the most objective and detached perspective each can muster about his or her own situation. The questions may address the nature of a partner's reactivity. Often such dialogue between the clinician and a spouse allows the listening partner to hear, perhaps for the first time, the other's views and thoughts about matters important to both. It is not uncommon for one or the other to comment "I never knew he (she) thought that." Spouses frequently look forward to the sessions as an opportunity to hear more about the other's point of view.

Additional effort can be directed toward engaging each partner's thinking and observations of the automatic emotional patterns that characterize their relationship. Often small emotional expressions in one produce intense responses in the other. A tone of voice, a particular glance or set of the mouth, and the angle at which one carries one's head are but a few of these subtle emotional stimuli or triggers. Sometimes the trigger will be so aversive that the other will do anything to avoid it. On the other hand the stimulus can be so pleasurable that the other will go to great lengths to provoke it. If spouses can become better observers of such patterns and stimuli, they can acquire an understanding of their own reactivity. The effort to observe the patterns and triggers can actually lower reactivity.

KEEPING SELF DETRIANGLED FROM THE FAMILY EMOTIONAL PROCESS

The effort to detriangle oneself from the family emotional oneness is equivalent to the effort to remain neutral in the family. There are innumerable ways in which the clinician takes sides, often without ever saying a word. This is no different from the many ways in which he or she took sides in the emotional issues of his or her parents. When one takes sides, one has joined the emotional process in the family. The effort to remain emotionally neutral is the central, most challenging task for the clinician in working with a family.

The emotional process between two people or two parties is continually reaching out to involve a third. This is the essence of the concept of the triangle described in Chapter 2. Yet the emotional intensity between two people will resolve itself automatically if a third person can remain in active contact with each of them while remaining outside the emotional field between them (Bowen, 1966, 1971). This is the theoretical basis for the effort to remain neutral.

In therapy, each spouse will attempt to involve the therapist in the family emotional system. While the mechanisms vary from person to person and family to family, it is predictable that such a move will be made. Each person will use what he or she has successfully used to involve others. The therapist has lost neutrality as completely when he or she is charmed as when angered.

It is difficult to communicate to others the nature and scope of the task that faces the clinician. Emotional participation is basic to all relationships. It may even play a significant role in the sustenance of life itself in the organism. Human emotional responsiveness ranges from subtle physiological change to the overt manifestations of conflict or romance. In short, it is natural for one human being to respond emotionally to another. The clinician is being asked to be aware of and to govern this natural response.

The effort to remain neutral is essentially impossible if the clinician focuses upon the surface or content issues in the family. Such topics can be produced at will. They rise, like the phoenix, from the apparent resolution of the immediately preceding issue. General themes of content include sex, money, and children and focus on issues of right or wrong, fairness, and rights. The family seeks continually to involve the clinician in such matters of content.

In contrast, emotional flow and patterns of reactivity become observable only when the therapist can find a relatively objective, neutral position from which to relate to the family. From such a position, like the quiet observer of a mountain pond, the therapist can see the ripples and vortices of emotionality that characterize family reactivity. The use of distance and its effects upon others can be seen. Triangles come into focus.

Bowen (1971) comments on a position that is neither too close nor too distant from the emotional process of the family. From that point he is able to watch the emotional flow and view the process without becoming entangled. He is able to comment either seriously or with humor. Such flexibility is the hallmark of the neutral or detriangled therapist. It is not what the therapist says that has primary importance. If he or she is caught in the family emotional system, almost anything the therapist says produces heightened reactivity in the family. When he or she is neutral and in contact, the clinician automatically says the right thing to aid thought and reduce anxiety. Often a casual comment stressing light humor can dissolve the tension of an overly serious presentation. Yet the pursuit of humor can mark the therapist's own emotional reactivity to the family. The ideal is to relate to the emotionally difficult areas for the family without becoming a part of the emotional system.

TEACHING THE FUNCTIONING OF EMOTIONAL SYSTEMS

Teaching about emotional systems is a natural part of assisting people to think about their situation and to control their reactivity. Timing plays an important role in the teaching effort. If teaching is attempted when anxiety is high, there are considerable disadvantages. Anxious people have a hard time listening fully to what is being said. Concepts can be partially heard and greatly misunderstood. The family can come back and say "We tried what you said and it didn't work," even though the therapist had not suggested any course of action. Somehow in the clinician's effort to explain an idea or concept, the family has heard a concrete step or technique. In another common variation, anxious spouses hear the material differently. They then go home and debate the point. On their return, they expect the therapist to indicate who heard correctly.

In the early course of therapy and at other times when anxiety is high, the therapist teaches by example. Frequently this involves the communication of positions for self, or I-positions, which will be described more fully in the next section. Stories can help make a point that could not be heard if directly stated. When anxiety is low, it is possible to present concepts directly in a neutral fashion. At such times it is much easier for family members to hear the ideas and consider them thoughtfully.

DEMONSTRATING THE I-POSITION DURING THE COURSE OF THERAPY

The pressures toward togetherness operate between the clinician and family members just as within the family itself. When a person can state his or her convictions and principles clearly and then act in accordance with such beliefs, it is possible for the togetherness pressures to abate. In communicating and acting upon such a position, the therapist does not imply criticism of the family nor does he or she become involved in an emotionally driven debate. This is the essence of the I-position.

In the early therapy sessions, when anxiety is high, the therapist relies frequently on the I-position to define him- or herself to the family. Each family member expects the therapist to act in a certain way or to relate in a specific manner. Such expectations are a part of the family emotional process. Some people expect the therapist to agree with their viewpoint or critique of self or another. Others act in a manner to force the therapist to follow an established course of action or accept some sort of responsibility for another. At such points it is necessary for the therapist to define him- or herself clearly and solidly to the family. It remains a continual task for the therapist to define self to the family whenever necessary and appropriate.

An I-position can be as simple as stating "I'm listening to your words, but I don't agree with what you're saying." Often such comments are made when a family member is attempting to persuade a clinician to see a content issue from a non-neutral perspective. More complex and intense situations producing an I-position occur around pressures for or against hospitalization, suicidal threat or gestures, and a range of other efforts or pressures upon the clinician to behave in a manner that goes against his basic principles and responsibilities.

The I-position is often viewed as a technique and applied frequently to whatever situation has produced an emotional response in the therapist. The heart of the I-position, however, is a movement for self, not for the family. In the author's experience, the I-position requires clear definition of responsibility presented at times when anxiety is pressing one toward irresponsibility. Over time the therapist can come to know the routine sorts of situations that require an I-position. Yet the more anxious and reactive family members are, the more likely the clinician will be presented with a situation without clear precedent and which will test his or her ability to be a self.

The method of working with two spouses to clarify and resolve emotional dysfunction in a family continues to be an effective method of family therapy. It is not, however, the only method of Family Systems Therapy. In a 1974 paper, Bowen reported an accidental discovery that had major theoretical and methodological importance. In March 1967, Bowen described his efforts to differentiate a self in his own family at a national conference of family oriented clinicians. The ideas and work of twelve years, upon which the presentation was based, quickly began to enter Bowen's teaching at Georgetown. He began to focus in a different way on the triangle between self and parents.

From such observations and conclusions, there evolved another method of working in the family emotional system. Like the coach who works with an athlete to improve basic skills and ability, the therapist coaches the person toward differentiation of self. The coach functions more as a consultant and teacher than a therapist, at least in the conventional understanding of the term. Coaching frequently occurs with only one member of a family at a session, although at times others are seen as well. Progress comes from the efforts the individual makes towards differentiation of self in the family. The coach assists in the direction of the effort and with suggestions for avoiding pitfalls and roadblocks that inevitably occur.

Shortly after these changes entered the teaching process, Bowen noted that people in the training sessions began to use the concepts during visits to their own families. This was something new, and the teaching conferences were used to report such visits and to obtain suggestions for future work (Bowen, 1974). By late 1967 and early 1968, Bowen observed that residents who had participated in the teaching conferences were doing better clinical work in family therapy than previous residents, even those who had been involved in weekly therapy sessions with their spouses. Furthermore, the residents who had done the best work with their original families were also doing the best clinical work. Yet another discovery occurred about a year later, when Bowen began to ask about the residents' emotional adjustment with their own spouses and children. He learned that they were automatically transferring what they had learned in the work with their parents to the relationships in their nuclear families (Bowen, 1974).

None of these residents or their spouses was in therapy. The conferences in which they participated were didactic and not designed to be therapeutic. The actual time spent with any individual was only a few minutes every other month or so. Yet these people were making faster progress than any others, including those in private therapy. Bowen's conclusion was

> that families in which the focus is on the differentiation of self in the families of origin automatically make as much or more progress in working out the relationship system with spouses and children as families seen in formal family therapy in which there is a principal focus on the interdependence in the marriage (Bowen, 1974, pp. 83–84).

The practical aspects of coaching are quite different from those of traditional individual therapy. Sessions are generally infrequent, often once a month or at even greater intervals. People well-schooled and experienced in the effort to increase differentiation of self may be seen yearly or on an as needed basis. The focus is primarily on the family of origin, and there may be little or no discussion of nuclear family relationships. The responsibility for the effort remains with the individual and not with the coach.

The following general directions guide the work within the family of origin: (1) an effort to become a more accurate observer of self and the family; (2) the development of person-to-person relationships with each member of the family; (3) an effort to increase one's ability to control emotional reactivity to the family; and (4) a sustained effort to remain neutral or detriangled while relating to the emotional issues of the family.

BECOMING AN ACCURATE OBSERVER AND CONTROLLING REACTIVITY

Becoming an accurate observer of oneself and of the family and attaining increased control of one's own emotional reactivity are interconnected assignments (Bowen, 1974). The effort to become more observant automatically detaches a person a little from the emotional process in the family. What one initially attempts to note is the sensitivity of people to one another. Of particular importance is one's own sensitivity and reactivity. It is necessary to observe carefully, for reactivity is often subtle. The effort to observe self and others carefully, however, often aids the related task of controlling one's own reactivity.

An outcome of this effort can be greater objectivity for the observer. The more objective one becomes, the more difficult it is to take sides in the family. It becomes possible to understand emotionally that no one is to blame for what happens in the family. When one can understand emotionally that everyone plays a part, including oneself, it is hard to be angry at anyone.

DEVELOPMENT OF PERSON-TO PERSON RELATION-SHIPS

The idea of a person-to-person relationship would appear to be so well understood that no further explanation is required. Yet many people find, when they think about it more carefully, that they lack a working understanding of the nature of a person-to-person relationship. Bowen defined what he meant by the term in the following manner. "In broad terms, a person-to-person relationship is one in which two people can relate personally to each other about each other, without talking about others (triangling), and without talking about impersonal things" (Bowen, 1974, p. 79). People are generally unable to stay on this kind of personal level for very long. Usually within a few seconds the conversation will shift to someone else or to an impersonal topic like the weather.

The effort to establish a person-to-person relationship to all living members of one's extended family is an exercise in developing maturity and perspective. It requires that a person recognize and master all the behaviors and feelings that work against the ability to relate to another on a personal level. The nature of this effort differs among individuals. For the author, it quickly illuminates the various mechanisms used to insulate self from others. It draws attention to the physiological indicators of reactivity that surface when an attempt is made to relate personally to an important other. Although the effort and learning are primarily for self, the relationship system may benefit from such an effort.

A variation of the effort to relate personally to each member of the family is the development of a person-to-person relationship with each parent. This is particularly difficult for people to understand. Many people have carefully structured their relationships to parents to preserve calm congeniality. Relating occurs on the basis of roles long established in the family. It is easy, in such a structured, pleasant situation, to believe that one has a personal relationship to each parent. Yet the roles and the atmosphere work as effectively against knowing the other on a personal level as do conflict and distance. Where a person has maintained a distant and tense relationship to parents, he or she tends to be aware of the discomfort and intensity of the relationship.

The effort to build a personal relationship with each parent is difficult. A coach who has worked on the task in his or her own family can be invaluable. There are numerous blind alleys and roadblocks that can stop an effort, sometimes for years. The emotional problems that have existed between the parents and in their relationships to their own extended families become clear and at times lively. The coach can provide suggestions for navigating such unknown and sometimes troubled waters.

REMAINING NEUTRAL

The effort to detriangle oneself from emotional situations in the family has already been discussed earlier in the chapter. In the effort to differentiate a self in one's own family, attention must be paid to interlocking triangles that come alive with each effort. One can seemingly be progressing in a given triangle only to lose ground when an emotional onslaught comes from an unexpected quarter. People who want to join self are as problematic as those who set out to prove one wrong. An effort to increase differentiation is conducted by self for self. There is no substitute for the continued effort in one's own family to learn about triangles.

In an effort to differentiate a self, frequent contact with other family members is important, particularly when anxiety is high. Generally something is gained in face-to-face contact, especially during periods of high anxiety in the family. Common events that can elevate family anxiety include periods of illness, births, marriages, deaths, and funerals. The individual is generally better off if she or he goes alone to see family members. Spouses and children are obviously important people, yet their presence can result in the family member's relating to them and eluding the person-to-person effort. Telephone and postal contact can also be useful.

A common dilemma awaiting the unwary concerns the notion of getting to know the family better. Contacts with family at group occasions, for example reunions, often produce a surge of positive, warm emotional response. It is difficult to have a position for self that threatens the warm closeness. Another variant is the family "encounter group." The idea is to get the family together to talk about the problems. Such meetings can occasionally clear the air temporarily and may provide some tension relief. It does not contribute toward differentiation and can move the family toward greater emotional reactivity. If sufficient emotional intensity is produced in such a group experience, the outcome can be explosive emotional reactivity and major disruption of relationships in the family.

Bowen (1974) cautions that one cannot tell the family what one is trying to do and still make it work. Family members may want to help out or may disagree with one's plan. Either way the differentiating effort can be stalled. Natural forces of resistance can build into an insurmountable roadblock. When one can have some control over emotional reactivity, however, he or she becomes important to everyone in the family. Some ability to control reactivity allows a degree of choice. One can participate and freely react to the emotional network around self.

Yet one always has the ability to slow down the reactivity and become more observant.

References

Bowen, M. (1966). The use of family theory in clinical practice. *Comprehensive Psychiatry, 7,* 345-374.

Bowen, M. (1971). Family therapy and family group therapy. In H. Kaplan & B. Sadock (Eds.), *Comprehensive group psychotherapy* (pp. 384-421). Baltimore: Williams and Wilkens.

Bowen, M. (1974). Toward the differentiation of self in one's family of origin. In P. Lorio & F. Andres (Eds.), *Georgetown family symposia* (Vol. 1, pp. 70-86). Washington, DC: Georgetown University Medical Center.

Bowen, M. (1976). Theory in the practice of psychotherapy. In P. Guerin (Ed.), *Family therapy* (pp. 42-90). New York: Gardner Press.

Chapter 5

A Clinical Situation: The "B" Family

A descriptive report of work with a family can be valuable to the serious student of theory and psychotherapy. At its best, a good report illustrates the linking of theory with practice. At its worst, it presents an oversimplified view of a few techniques essentially divorced from a theoretical context. The reading of one or many reports cannot substitute for the hours of work on theoretical questions and the additional hours of experience that form the basis of clinical excellence.

Bowen Family Systems Theory suggests that a family has the ability to manage its own problems if anxiety can be lowered and if at least one family member can begin to work toward a responsible position for self in relationship to important others in the family. The clinician aims to manage him- or herself in a manner that allows the family to become less anxious and to begin the process of deciding their own destiny.

With present technology it is not possible to enter the thinking process of another. There is no way to read the clinician's thoughts as he or she sits with a family in a clinical session. Yet how the clinician thinks is far more important than what is said or done. In a general sense the coach does not plan and implement interventions. It would be very difficult to look at a videotape of a clinical session and note a clinician's particular comment or action that made a special difference. One could say that the clinician works to maintain a level of differentiation of self in the presence of the family at all times. Yet to someone who has not worked to understand the concept of differentiation, very little is conveyed in such a statement.

The concept of differentiation addresses the sensitivity of individuals to one another and the automatic feeling states and responses such sensitivity produces. It focuses on the instinctual or emotional ways organisms attempt to create and maintain specific levels of closeness and distance to manage the discomfort of such reactivity. The clinician is always working to understand and contain his or her own reactivity to the family. He or she aims to maintain a perspective of inquiry, seeking more to understand the family and its dilemma rather than to act as an expert in solving family problems. Each family becomes another opportunity to learn more about human behavior in a family. When the clinician can maintain his or her autonomy in the presence of the family and a spirit of curious inquiry, he or she is on course.

The following report is drawn from the author's clinical experience. It has been selected because the family faced a difficult and serious problem that had attracted the attention of a range of professional clinicians. It illustrates the ability of a family to deal with intense issues thoughtfully and to remain on a self-determined course in spite of numerous obstacles.

CASE HISTORY

In November 1980, Mr. and Mrs. B were referred for family therapy by a clinical psychologist on the Mental Health Service of a large metropolitan hospital. The psychologist had been seeing Mr. B individually. Mr. B was a patient at the hospital in treatment for Hodgkin's disease. His medical team referred him to Dr. M, the clinical psychologist, when Mr. B showed symptoms of depression. Mr. B reacted intensely to injections, becoming nauseous and displaying panic. He had consequently, in effect, ended his chemotherapy. He was lethargic and indicated he no longer cared what happened to him. During the course of his individual therapy, Mr. B asked if he could be seen together with his wife. Dr. M also came to believe that the tension between Mr. and Mrs. B merited attention and made the referral.

In November 1980, when family therapy sessions began, the B family was in a tight spot. Mr. B was fully aware of his treatment team's opinion that continued chemotherapy was necessary. He was also aware of his wife's concerns about his health and about the future of the family if he should die without making what preparations he could for their well-being. For her part, Mrs. B was faced with her husband's withdrawal from treatment and the anxiety such behavior produced in her.

During the initial session, Mrs. B indicated that she was very concerned about her husband's health and his refusal to continue treatment. She had tried everything she knew to urge him to carry on and had met with no success. She believed that he no longer loved her and indicated she did not know what to do about the situation. Mr. B simply stated he no longer cared about himself or the situation.

The initial sessions included the development of a family history and a history of the presenting problem. On two occasions, other family members were seen. In December 1980, Mr. B's mother was seen with Mr. and Mrs. B. She happened to be in town for the holidays and was willing to attend. In January 1981, the older daughter, C, attended once with her parents. This followed her losing a job through apparently irresponsible behavior.

Mr. and Mrs. B were seen together at all meetings except when, later, Mr. B was too ill to attend. A number of factors guide a decision to see people together or separately. The Bs had asked to be seen together. Furthermore it quickly became apparent in the clinical sessions that each was interested in what the other had to say. Each had the ability to restrain the urge to debate and argue, and each reported that the sessions together seemed to have a calming affect on the situation.

Factual information about the family was collected and recorded using a family diagram during the early sessions. That information is summarized in the following paragraphs and illustrated with the family diagram (see Figure 5-1).

Mr. B was born in 1935 in an Eastern state. He was the eldest of two sons, eight years older than his sibling. Both his mother and his brother were living in the same Eastern state in close proximity to one another. (The B family was living in a Southern state.) Mr. B's father had died in 1977. Mr. B maintained limited contact with his family. Mrs. B took much of the initiative in writing and calling her mother-in-law.

Mr. B had retired after twenty years of military service in 1974. He continued his career in private industry. In 1976, Hodgkin's disease was diagnosed. From that point on he was rarely free from some sort of illness. Following five months hospitalization in the spring of 1977 for treatment of Hodgkin's disease, Mr. B developed a serious case of histoplasmosis in the summer of 1977. He received chemotherapy that continued to the spring of 1978. For the next year Mr. B did relatively well. The Hodgkin's disease was in remission, and he was free of other ailments. In December 1979, the symptoms of Hodgkin's disease reappeared, leading to a six-month period of chemotherapy. In January 1980, he also received radiation therapy. In March 1980, he was hospitalized once more for adult chicken pox. It was at this point that Mr. B refused further chemotherapy and began his course of therapy with Dr. M.

Mrs. B was born in Germany in 1939. She is the second of three children and the second daughter. Her older sister and younger brother remained in Germany along with her parents when Mrs. B moved to the United States. Mrs. B's mother died in 1969 and her father less than a

The "B" Family

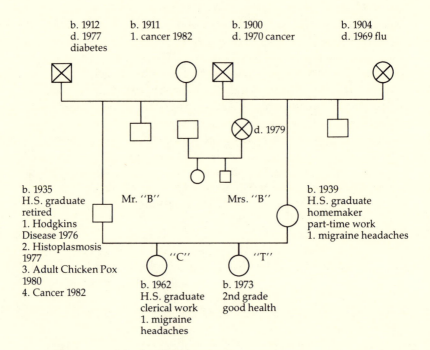

b. 1912
d. 1977
diabetes

b. 1911
1. cancer 1982

b. 1900
d. 1970 cancer

b. 1904
d. 1969 flu

d. 1979

b. 1935
H.S. graduate
retired
1. Hodgkins
Disease 1976
2. Histoplasmosis
1977
3. Adult Chicken Pox
1980
4. Cancer 1982

Mr. "B"

Mrs. "B"

b. 1939
H.S. graduate
homemaker
part-time work
1. migraine headaches

"C"

"T"

b. 1962
H.S. graduate
clerical work
1. migraine
headaches

b. 1973
2nd grade
good health

Chronology of Mr. B's health:

1. 1976 - Hodgkins Disease diagnosed
2. 1977 (spring) - 5 months hospitalization for Hodgkins
3. 1977 (summer) - histoplasmosis
4. 1977-1978 (fall to spring) - chemotherapy
5. 1978-1979 - clinical remission of Hodgkins Disease
6. 1980 (winter to spring) - chemotherapy for Hodgkins Disease
7. 1980 (May) - adult chicken pox
8. 1980 (summer to early fall) - refuses further chemotherapy
9. 1980 (November) - begin family therapy
10. 1981 (spring) - clinical remission
11. 1981 (June) - testicular mass
12. 1981-1982 - histoplasmosis (hospitalized)
13. 1982 (spring) - neurological difficulties
14. 1982 (July) - cancer

Figure 5.1 The "B" Family Diagram

year later in 1970. In April 1979, her older sister was killed in an automobile accident. Mrs. B reported that loss as significant to her. She had relied a great deal on her sister for emotional support across time. She remained in reasonably good contact with members of her family in Europe by letter and the exchange of audio tapes, although following the death of her sister she found it difficult to let family members know of her own troubles. She indicated that she did not wish to burden them unnecessarily with her problems.

Mr. and Mrs. B were married in 1961 after a fourteen-month courtship. They met in West Germany, where Mr. B was stationed with the Air Force. In 1962, their older daughter, C, was born. Over the next ten years, the family moved to England and then to the United States. In 1973, their second daughter, T, was born. Both children were and continue to be in good health. Mr. and Mrs. B tended to worry some about C. She appeared to lack direction in life and at times would function with apparent irresponsibility. Mrs. B saw her as lacking in motivation and not living up to her potential.

Mrs. B is a bright, energetic woman. Her characteristic approach to life is to work very hard at what she undertakes. She characterized herself as striving to see the good in all situations and to maintain a sense of humor. She has been a primary force in the family. Mr. B commented during the early sessions that "she has always been my backbone." For his part, Mr. B was a reserved, thoughtful, and at times witty man. In most situations he would appear to defer to Mrs. B's opinions and decisions. Over the twenty-plus years of marriage, Mrs. B managed most family endeavors. At times she had experimented in leaving important projects to Mr. B. Experience, however, had taught her to handle most things herself. Mr. B agreed that he tended to be unreliable on many family projects.

CLINICAL ANALYSIS

From the factual information collected and from discussions with the Bs, the following picture emerged of the family's immediate dilemma and the emotional processes that contributed to it. The immediate crisis rovolved around Mr B's state of functional collapse. He was no longer bringing his own best thinking and capabilities to bear on the situation confronting him. Mr. and Mrs. B both reported similar situations when his functioning had slumped. In such situations he would defer to Mrs. B, who would act to straighten matters out. This functional decline exceeded any previous one, and Mrs. B was unable to take effective charge of the situation. In a sense, therefore, she too, was unable to function.

The notion of functional collapse contains at least two levels of meaning. In the first place, it conveys that the functioning of the individual or unit has declined to the point of apparent helplessness. In addition the notion implies that the dysfunction is somehow functional for the individual or unit. It can be thought of as the response of the person to environmental incursions that have routed his or her more usual means of adapting and adjusting to changing conditions. Among the foremost of environmental incursions is the anxious behavior of those people with whom the person must interact. At times, for Mr. B, anxious others would include helping professionals and members of his family upon whom he was dependent. Generally the anxious environment believes it knows what is best for the individual or unit and attempts to convince or coerce compliance.

Mrs. B was fully aware of her husband's functional collapse. She was trying her best to motivate him and move him along. She was receiving anxiety from Mr. B's treatment team, who talked to her about their concerns and urged her to "help" Mr. B see the light about his treatments. The severity of his collapse added further anxiety. Aware that he might soon die, she worried that no preparations had been made for her and the children in the event of his death. In the face of these worries and anxieties, Mrs. B appeared to intensify her efforts to prop up and encourage Mr. B's functioning. She scolded, cajoled, and wept at times. Mr. B seemed impervious to these actions and retreated further.

This interactional pattern of pressure and retreat appears often in the family unit and illustrates the apparent helplessness each person experiences. Neither knows what to do about the other. In spite of evidence that the various efforts to influence the other to stop what he or she is doing are ineffective, each reacts with increasing intensity to the intransigence of the other. It is akin to the situation of the auto driver who, mired in the snow, applies increasing power to the drive wheels, virtually eliminating the ability of the tires to grip the surface and provide traction. In the case of a family, the driving force is anxiety. The higher the anxiety in each person and in the unit, the greater the tendency to "spin the wheels."

The information from the family diagram also provided a view of the operation of family emotional processes over time that may have contributed to the development of the situation in which the Bs were mired in the fall of 1980. The most critical process is emotional cutoff.

Mr. B maintained, as an adult, a relatively large degree of distance from his own family. He had left home as a young man and entered the military. Although he would occasionally visit his family when on leave, it was difficult for him to communicate about himself to them. After marriage, Mr. B left it to his wife to arrange infrequent visits and maintain regular contact with his relatives. Nevertheless, he remained sensitive emotionally to the family. During his illness, he often wept when talking to his mother on the telephone. With the distance from his family, Mrs. B became the center of his emotional life. When she was relatively calm and functioning well, his world was smooth. When she was anxious, however, his course was bumpy.

The reader will recall the earlier discussion of differentiation of self and emotional cutoff. The cutoff from emotionally significant others can be seen as a retreat from an emotional tide that threatens to erode the perceived autonomy and comfort of the person. It both solves a problem in the short run and creates a dilemma in the long run. The pressure to cutoff comes both from other people and from the person him- or herself. The more intense the cutoff, the more vulnerable the individual is to anxiety. He or she also tends to look for another to create another intense relationship matching that with the original family. While the person craves the intensity of closeness, he or she is also exquisitely sensitive to shifts in the other, making the new relationship rocky and difficult to maintain.

For Mr. B, the distance from his family (actual miles from his parental family and internally from his immediate family) appeared to work well initially. He was able to function reasonably in a military career, although from time to time his functioning would drop in the family. The distance from his original family heightened his sensitivity and reactivity to his spouse. In spite of his apparent functioning, he remained vulnerable to surges of anxiety that could lead to rapid drops in his functioning.

On a theoretical level, the functioning shift can be seen as more than behavioral. Theory suggests that the organism itself responds, leading potentially to changes in health and physical well-being. Mr. B's medical condition worsened considerably during the last months of his father's life (1977) and again following the death of Mrs. B's sister in 1979. His condition dramatically worsened following his mother's diagnosis of cancer in 1981, as the following narrative will describe. In short, the emotional cutoff with its unresolved sensitivity and reactivity appears to have played a role in Mr. B's health.

Although Mrs. B was in somewhat better contact with her family, she and the family appeared still to be adjusting to the death of her older sister unexpectedly in 1979. Following her parents' deaths in 1969 and 1970, Mrs. B had relied greatly on her sister as a supportive confidante and advisor. With the remainder of her family somewhat more distant, the loss of her sister left Mrs. B without natural mechanisms upon which she had relied for her own functioning. She saw no workable way to draw upon her family as a resource. She reported that she had not been able to tell her family about her own dilemma, because she did not want to add to their burden.

With her own anxiety very high and without the availability of natural family mechanisms to aid her, Mrs. B was having difficulty bringing her best faculties and resources to bear on the situation confronting her. In the past she had been able to take charge when Mr. B underfunctioned and straighten matters out. Now that mechanism seemed no longer to work. In fact it appeared to be making the situation worse. The level of anxiety in the family exceeded the capacity of the overfunctioning-underfunctioning reciprocity to manage it. In addition, both extended families were having their own difficulties adjusting to the emergence of new problems and dilemmas.

In summary, Mr. and Mrs. B appeared to be people with modest levels of differentiation of self. They had managed their own tensions with a reciprocal exchange of functioning in which Mr. B tended to lose functional differentiation and Mrs. B gained functional differentiation. Now conditions were changing more rapidly and with greater impact than existing mechanisms for managing anxiety could handle. The changes were occurring both within their own nuclear family and in both extended families. The outcome was the functional collapse of both Mr. and Mrs. B.

ANALYSIS OF METHODOLOGY

The clinician followed the basic methodology outlined in the preceding chapter for working with spouses. He spoke with each directly, asking questions, and occasionally giving suggestions or stating his own views. Often he attempted to spend the first thirty minutes with one while the other listened. Then the positions were reversed in the final thirty minutes. His goals were relatively simple. He would try to have enough control of his own anxiety that he could relate to the family about any emotional subject without reacting and taking sides in the emotional processes within the family and between the family and the treatment team. From this relatively neutral but in-contact position he would try to tap the clearest thinking each could muster about the situation and the emotional issues in the family. From a longer-range perspective, if anxiety could decrease and functioning improve, it might be possible for one or both to regain better contact with extended family, bringing natural mechanisms into play. Even longer range might be the possibility that one or both could begin the difficult effort to define a self.

Perhaps an example may illustrate the kind of activity involved. The clinician asked Mrs. B a range of questions related to her own functioning and how she viewed the situation. What was helpful, what not? What seemed to be preventing her becoming a more effective helper? How did she explain that? Occasionally during the sessions, tears would form in her eyes. At such times the clinician would ask her about the nature of the thoughts that preceded the tears and how she accounted for such an impact. The thinking process never faltered during these periods, and often Mrs. B reported in later sessions that she had been able to think much more clearly about the particular situation following such episodes.

With Mr. B the questions were fewer, often asking only for his thoughts as he had listened to his spouse. When he had a comment, low-key questions followed to clarify and amplify his thought. No effort was made to convince him to accept treatment. Only one question was directed to his functioning (at least during the early sessions). What had he been doing to help his wife and daughters prepare for his death?

For most clinicians there is a strong urge to help. In addition a family can apply a great deal of pressure through the postures they assume and the "answers" they demand of the clinician. One of the difficult pressures for the clinician is the urge to take sides. It can come both from within and outside of self. The side-taking can be subtle or overt. Another pressure attempts to link the clinician's self esteem with the performance of the family. One is competent, a fine clinician, when the family appears to do what is "right." On the other hand one is incompetent or the family is "wrong" when it does not respond appropriately. The judgment about the clinician's abilities can come from within self, from the family, or from the broader environment. Yet the more the therapist can simply be in contact with the family without taking sides and without providing answers to the dichotomies of family emotionality, the greater the likelihood someone in the family can address the challenge of responsible functioning.

To be in contact with a family requires that one be close enough or connected sufficiently to the family system that one's presence has an effect. To avoid side-taking or providing answers requires the clinician to remain relatively differentiated from the family. Said differently, the clinician must have an awareness of and a degree of control over his or her own reactivity to the family.

In any situation like that confronting the B family the side-taking opportunities are endless. A major polarization concerned Mr. B and his treatment team. Another version of the same basic dilemma operated between Mr. and Mrs. B. A basic task for the clinician was to remain continually on neutral territory.

The author believed that if he could remain in contact with the family and relatively differentiated, anxiety could decrease sufficiently that the B family could find a way through its dilemmas. He believed that improved functioning might be observable in two areas. Mr. B could become a more active participant in his own treatment, more a partner with his physicians than solely the object of their concern and effort. In short, he could regain a degree of functioning and reduce the anxiety of his treatment team. Mrs. B could assume less responsibility for her husband's health care decisions and could find a way to make responsible decisions in regard to her own future and that of the family. There should also be a decrease in the level of marital conflict.

By early January, 1981 (after eight weekly sessions), the first reports of shift appeared. Mrs. B reported that she no longer was reacting intensely to Mr. B's episodes of "depressed" behavior at home. She reported she was better able to contain her urge to make things better for him and better able to recognize his tearful periods as a part of his dilemma. Mr. B reported that he was able to get beyond his tears more quickly when his wife reacted less intensely. By February 1981, Mrs. B reported that her husband had taken action on several matters related to the financial well-being of the family in the event of his death. She reported her own tension had considerably decreased.

The spring of 1981 marked a period of relatively good functioning for the family. Mr. B's Hodgkin's disease was once again in remission. He was active at home and in the community. Mrs. B reported greater activity of her own related to part-time employment and a generally brighter outlook on life. Mr. and Mrs. B continued to worry about C, now living at home, but reported that she, too, appeared to be getting her feet on the ground.

Mr. B's sensitivity to his family became readily apparent toward the late spring of 1981. During that period Mr. B's brother was briefly hospitalized for relief of emotional distress. In late spring, Mr. B's mother was diagnosed as having cancer, and she entered a public hospice to live out the progression of the disease. Although his functioning continued to be high, Mr. B reported great reactivity to the news from his family. He would cry when talking to them on the telephone. In May 1981, Mr. B traveled to visit his mother and brother. He spent a week with his family, and on the night before his return home, he noted pain in his groin. Subsequent medical examination revealed an previously undetected testicular mass.

His physicians recommended surgery to remove the mass. Mr. B participated fully in the discussions around the surgery and made the initial decision to delay the surgery pending the outcome of further observation and treatment. He appeared to be playing a major role in determining the direction of his medical care.

During the fall of 1981, Mr. B's health took a marked downturn. Although the Hodgkin's disease continued in remission, Mr. B was hospitalized for treatment of histoplasmosis. The course of treatment was difficult and long. At times it appeared Mr. B might not survive.

In spite of his condition, Mr. B did not lapse into helplessness. He knew his condition required chemotherapy. Aware of his intense reaction to injections, Mr. B agreed to the implantation of a Hickman catheter through which medications could be administered. Mr. B appeared to be actively interacting with his physician and contributing to his own care. His condition remained serious much of the winter, although he seemed to be improving gradually.

Mrs. B remained active during this period. She visited Mr. B frequently in the hospital and cared for him where she could. She learned many of the nursing care procedures required to maintain the Hickman catheter. She had an awareness of anxiety in herself and worked actively to contain her reactivity. During this time Mr. and Mrs. B reported a closeness that had not been present earlier in their marriage. They reported an increased ability to talk together about difficult issues and increased enjoyment of interaction with one another.

An important thrust of Mrs. B's effort to manage herself in the situation involved a continuing effort to define responsible helpfulness in the situation. How could she provide help her husband needed without becoming overly responsible nor doing too much. This is a significant challenge to anyone faced with a situation of this intensity. She was able essentially to maintain contact with Mr. B, providing necessary physical assistance. Yet somehow she was able to recognize that Mr. B's substantial mental capacity was not impaired and that he did not require her functioning for him in terms of decisions and in his relationships to other people. She was able to talk with him and listen to his thinking without attempting to make basic decisions for him.

During this period the clinician often saw Mrs. B alone when Mr. B was too ill or too uncomfortable to attend the sessions. Occasionally he saw Mr. B at his bedside when conditions allowed. Since both appeared to be managing anxiety rather well, the sessions focused on thinking about specific aspects of the broad situation. How did each see the situation and his or her own functioning in it? What sorts of changes were occurring, what was the evidence for that point of view, and how could it be accounted for? Both reported that between sessions they found themselves thinking about the questions raised and working out resolutions and decisions for themselves.

C's behavior continued to be a source of concern. Her functioning appeared to decrease as Mr. B's condition worsened. A turning point was reached in the early winter of 1982. C and a friend were involved in an automobile accident. While neither girl was seriously injured, considerable medical expenses were involved. There was no insurance on the vehicle, and Mr. and Mrs. B had to help cover the cost. Mr. and Mrs. B consulted about the situation, and Mrs. B handled it somewhat differently than on previous occasions. She worked to control her urge to lecture and complain to C about her behavior. She was able to make it clear to C that she would be expected to reimburse her parents for their expenses from her own small earnings. As time went by, Mrs. B was able to stick to her position, and C began repaying her debt. Following this episode, C's functioning appeared to improve slowly, although at times she and Mrs. B would occasionally come into conflict.

In the spring of 1982, Mr. B's condition improved sufficiently that he could go home from the hospital. Mrs. B took over some of the nursing care with the assistance of the hospital staff. In late spring, however, Mr. B began to lose the use of his legs. His health appeared to be worsening and at times his thinking capacities were diminished. He returned to the hospital for further medical workups. During this period the author saw Mrs. B at two- to three-week intervals. Mr. B participated when he was able. His condition slowly deteriorated.

FOLLOW-UP

In June 1982, the author left the medical center for a new position in another state. He discussed the situation with Mr. and Mrs. B and indicated that Dr. M was willing to see them if they wished. The decision, however, would be up to them. Mr. and Mrs. B both said they were sorry to see the author leave and wished him well. Mrs. B agreed to keep him informed of the family's progress. They decided not to continue with Dr. M. The following narrative is based on information supplied by Mrs. B.

Mr. B's condition steadily worsened during the summer of 1982. Bladder cancer was diagnosed, and Mr. B twice underwent surgery. Recurrent bladder infections were difficult to deal with medically. By late summer, Mr. B was very ill. Bone cancer was discovered, and the medical team recommended chemotherapy.

Mr. B participated in the discussion of this new development with his medical team. He was alert and asked intelligent questions indicating he understood the severity of the situation and the basis of the medical recommendation. He actively considered the options available to him and made his own decision.

Mrs. B describes his informing her of his decision in the following passage:

> I came in and George (Mr. B) said to me "Get me Dr. G. I don't want the chemotherapy. I've decided against it." And I said "OK, I will." He said "Do you hate me for what I'm doing?" I said "Honey, I've pushed all these years. I'm not going to push you now. If you want to take it, I'm here. I will help you...If you decide against it, that is fine. You do know, however, that you are not going to live much longer." He said "Yes, I am aware of that." I said "Do you want to die?" He said "I just want to be at peace...I want to be home. I want to get out of here. I want to be home with you." And I said "Alright, that's just where you'll be."

Mrs. B arranged to take her husband home. During the summer, C had functioned well and had been able to enter a military training program. When contacted by her mother, she took leave from the training program and returned home to help with her father's care. She continued to function well at home and took an active role in nursing her father.

Mr. B spent the last three weeks of his life at home. Mrs. B assumed responsibility for nursing care. C continued to assist her, and friends as well as a public health nurse made regular visits. Mrs. B maintained daily telephone contact with the hospital treatment team.

Mr. B's condition varied greatly. Sudden, often unforeseen changes occurred, and Mrs. B had to manage her own intense levels of anxiety. At such times she reports she would question the wisdom of her decision to support Mr. B's wish to die at home. At other times, well-meaning friends and medical personnel questioned her decision, creating moments of self-doubt and indecision. Each time she found a way to think clearly about the situation and the basis for her decision. She continued on the course she had chosen.

As his condition worsened, Mr. B moved in and out of contact with reality. During his clear moments he and Mrs. B would converse about matters important to them. He indicated to Mrs. B that he loved her and was grateful for her efforts to care for him at home. When Mr. B was confused, she was able to find ways to talk past the confusion to the person behind it and calm him. Both the B children saw their father daily and were involved in his care. Other relatives and friends were present from time to time. Mr. B cooperated as best he could. At times he found ways to inject humorous comments and observations, indicating his awareness of the situation and the interaction with others.

On September 19, 1982, Mr. B died at home. C was caring for him at the time, noticed his difficulty, and she summoned her mother. Mrs. B and C were with him when he died. Shortly after death, the younger daughter, T, came into the room and kissed and hugged her father.

At the time of writing, ten months have passed since Mr. B's death. Mrs. B reports that adjustment for her has not been easy. She maintains part-time employment and is thinking about her future. She reports that she has remained in regular contact with Mr. B's family as well as with several members of her own family. In addition she regularly visits the medical staff and other Hodgkin's patients with whom she became acquainted during Mr. B's long illness. She reports she remains secure in the decision she and Mr. B made in caring for him at home.

Mrs. B's relationship with C remains difficult. Following her father's death, C resumed her military career. In May, 1983, C married a military colleague. Mrs. B continues to be reactive to this decision. She reports, however, that C appears happy and functioning well. She has repaid her financial obligations to the family and remains in regular contact with her mother. C appears to be doing well in her military career.

Her younger sister, T, lives at home with Mrs. B. T is maintaining good grades in school and appears to be adjusting well. She and Mrs. B talk from time to time about Mr. B and the events around his death. T comments that she has her own memories of her father. An acquaintance inquired recently of Mrs. B how "T could be so happy a child with all that has been going on."

Mr. and Mrs. B each reported that the family therapy sessions were very useful. Each mentioned that it was possible to hear what the other was saying in a different and new way. It became possible to know the other differently than before. Each reported thinking about the sessions afterward and what had been said. Somehow that was helpful in formulating new ways of thinking and acting in old stalemates. Mrs. B reports that she continues to think about the sessions from time to time and gains clarity in her current thinking. She comments that during the last months of Mr. B's life they were happily closer than ever before. She attributes that happiness in part to the work in family therapy.

The functional collapse Mr. B displayed at the time family sessions began never returned. He continued up to his death to make as many of his own decisions as possible and to cooperate in an active manner with his physicians. Mrs. B reported an increased ability to think for herself about the situation and to reduce the pressure she had placed on Mr. B. During the course of family therapy C's functioning appeared to improve and to sustain itself through Mr. B's final illness and beyond.

Throughout the course of consultation with the B family, the clinician attempted only to remain in contact with the family and to maintain a relative level of differentiation from the family. No particular interventions were planned or implemented, although a range of feeling-laden issues were touched upon during the sessions.

If there is a magic to family therapy, it lies in the ability of families to manage the most difficult of situations. That magic is not the product of a particular intervention or even of a particular clinician. Any other individual who would work to remain in neutral contact with the B family and relatively differentiated could have been of as much assistance as the actual clinician. Once their level of anxiety decreased, Mr. and Mrs. B automatically began to function with higher levels of thought and responsibility.

The B family faced its dilemmas in a way that made sense to them and was consistent within each family member's definition of responsibility for self. The efforts to think each issue through for oneself and to reduce and control the sensitivity and reactivity to one another made their decisions workable. For another family the workable decision might involve hospital care of the dying person. Other families could come to very different resolutions of difficult dilemmas if someone in the family is willing to work on reducing his or her own reactivity and struggling to find a responsible stance for self in relationship to others. Both Mr. and Mrs. B "heard" that viewpoint and were able to make the effort involved.

Chapter 6
Training in Theory, Thought, and Therapy

New frontiers have always been a part of the human experience. For good and for ill, trailblazers have pointed the way toward dimly seen destinations. Such distant horizons are not easily dismissed, and humankind has pressed ahead. Slowly people have reached every portion of Earth and now aim to escape man's tether to the planet. The world of ideas also has been marked by the human tendency to press ahead. Some thinkers have moved far beyond the boundaries of the known world to new visions of what is and what might be. Science, knowledge of the facts of nature, owes much to such visionaries. Behind them have come legions of workers, collecting, testing, supporting, and disputing. Often the forerunner defines the problematic knot that the successful worker then unravels, becoming in the process a visionary him- or herself.

A theory is a formal statement of vision in the realm of science. Theory belongs to the realm of scientific endeavor, the effort to learn facts of nature. While clearly not science, good theory rests upon scientific fact. At its best, theory is a bridge of thought connecting facts, implying a relationship among them. John B. Calhoun, in a recent address, made a distinction between what he called *rich* and *minimal theories*. A rich theory encompasses many parameters and a broad range of ideas. It is therefore difficult to investigate but can lead to new areas of research and discovery. A minimal theory, on the other hand, focuses on the smallest unit that can be definitively managed. It can be easily investigated and yields rapid but limited results.

Therapy is a by-product of theory. It is an eddy in the forward rush of thinking and knowledge. A rich theory can spin off many therapies in different arenas. The value of each is limited and subject to drastic change as new knowledge leads to new discoveries that supersede the old. Skilled practitioners can contribute a great deal therapeutically. But, in the long run, therapy is only as good as the science upon which it rests.

Bowen Family Systems Theory is rich with ideas and potential. As a theory, it is always subject to revision and refinement. New discoveries in any pertinent realm of scientific endeavor can lead to modifications. Representing a new way of thinking about the human, it challenges its supporters to specify ever more precisely what is meant and what its implications are. At the same time, its richness leads thinkers and practitioners to press ahead into new regions of thought and action. The goal is expanded knowledge, a new science.

Science, theory, and therapy are communicated through the process of training. One generally assumes that training involves the transfer of information or skill from someone who knows to another who does not. Yet the effort to convey theory and thinking to someone else ultimately highlights both the known and the unknown. An effective training effort produces new questions and problems to be solved. Gaps in knowledge and reasoning become clearer than otherwise. The instructor must take care not to present knowledge in a manner that disguises gaps and presumes all questions have been answered. In such a context learning can become rote and curiosity dampened. The teacher can be overvalued (or overblamed), and the learner may miss the important, even essential, insight that he or she has in the final responsibility for personal learning. At the same time, the instructor must convey the basics of thinking in a way that allows the learner to move ahead.

Training in family theory and therapy varies greatly. It may be highly experiential, with role play and live supervision of clinical work. Other formats include lectures, seminars, and required readings to fill out the training regimen. Precisely what is to be taught or communicated in a training program is also varied. How much attention should be paid to theory and how much to the techniques of therapy? If one believes that the basics of human functioning are well understood and clear, then one can attempt to train people in techniques that fit any given situation in a family. If one believes that such knowledge is currently at best rudimentary, then training might aim to develop thinkers and explorers who can advance knowledge. Such issues and questions bedevil anyone who must address matters of training and learning.

Theory is central to training in Bowen Family Systems ideas. Family Systems Theory is based on a new, different view of the human. Students of theory must move beyond conventional notions of human behavior. But how can one learn to see what one has never seen before? What motivates a person to press ahead into the unknown toward a new understanding? How does a faculty communicate the importance of theory and thinking in a manner that aids one to see without creating a new blindness? These are central questions when considering an effort to communicate family theory to another.

Because Bowen Family Systems Theory is a theory about the human and human functioning, a member of the faculty is expected not only to talk about theory but to embody it. At the heart of Bowen Family Systems Theory lies the concept of differentiation of self. A faculty member can never address him- or herself sufficiently to the concept of differentiation, not only in what he or she says but in how he or she functions. On a broad level differentiation takes up the manner in which organisms differ from one another in terms of sensitivity and automatic or instinctual response to the environment. An important direction in training involves the effort to learn about one's own sensitivity and automatic responsiveness. The learner also aims to develop a degree of control over the automatic nature of the response.

Frequently the task of learning about differentiation is framed in terms of the distinction between the emotional and the intellectual or cognitive systems of the individual. The term *emotional system* has a specific connotation. The emotional system incorporates the processes generally called feelings but is believed to be much broader and more fundamental than feelings. The emotional system is identical to the instinctual system, the automatic internal guidance system of the organism. All life-forms have some sort of emotional system. The intellectual system refers to the capacity of the organism to observe itself and its environment, to reflect upon or think about its observations, and to influence its response on the basis of such reflection.

The distinction between thought and emotion is elusive. It might be clearer if one could imagine a continuum. At one end would be pure emotional system activity and at the other end pure intellectual activity. Toward the emotional end of the continuum would fall behaviors like a mother's response to a distress cry from her child, the panic of a crowd in a burning theater, and the behaviors associated with romantic passion. At the other end might come behaviors like the efforts of a scientist to make his or her own mental processes more objective. Paranoia, jealousy, and other similar feeling and behavior states could be seen as products of emotional system functioning, even though in the human they involve mental processes.

One could also address differentiation in terms of subjectivity and objectivity. To be sure no product of the human brain is completely objective. All information must pass through the sensory nerve network to the completely enclosed brain, which has no direct link with the world outside the skull. Nevertheless one can distinguish between the self-centeredness of subjectivity and a broader, more balanced perspective called objectivity. In a subjective mode the human defines self as different from all others, is acutely aware of the impact of others on self, and operates as if one were the center of the universe and the judge of all that occurs. Objectivity appreciates the similarity of living forms, is mindful of the influence of self on another, and is aware of one's dependency on all other living things and on the earth itself.

Each person's understanding of differentiation of self tends to differ somewhat from that of another. Although a great deal can be learned from the families one sees professionally, the clinician's own family is a most productive teacher. Faculty members, therefore, are expected to spend time learning about their families and their own sensitivity to important family members. Here formulas for observation, objectivity, and fact are forged and tested. Basic lessons in respect for family emotional process are brought home unforgettably. The learning from such efforts becomes an important element in a faculty member's effort to represent differentiation of self.

In addition to representing differentiation of self, a faculty member is expected to be familiar with and to apply what is called systems thinking. The preceding chapters, in essence, have attempted to describe some of the details of systems thinking. In general, however, it is characterized by a broad rather than a narrow perspective. Instead of breaking phenomena into parts for analysis, the systems thinker attempts to see the operation of wholes and how pieces fit with one another. Secondly, a systems thinker is always aware of and interested in the effect he has on the phenomenon observed. The observer becomes a part of the system.

The instructor's effort in training resembles the work with clinical families. Any individual, as a representative of a family, presents an opportunity to learn more about the human. The goal for the instructor is to be in contact with the thinking of the learner without responding emotionally to it. The goal for the learner is to move toward greater differentiation of self. In this process, both parties are in fact learning. Each challenges the other to think for him- or herself.

It is difficult to assess an individual's level of differentiation of self on a short-term basis. Work and experience in training represent only a beginning. What can be reasonably expected, however, is that the learner will have developed a working understanding of the concept that allows him or her to continue the effort toward differentiation on into the future. One can also expect that the learner will have developed a way to recognize his or her own undifferentiation in the family of origin, the family in which he or she lives, and in the families seen in clinical practice.

A necessary quality in both teacher and learner is a curiosity about the nature of human behavior and the problems families face. Although one can broadly generalize about families and problems, each family sees itself as unique. And to a degree each family is different, and each problem is an opportunity for the clinician to learn. To see that opportunity in any family is a challenge to both the experienced as well as the inexperienced therapist.

An important question can frequently act as the catalyst to thinking and ultimately seeing. Good questions beg solutions and lead to appreciation of complexity and sophistication in understanding. What is an important question? It must, in the first place, be a serious question. It must touch upon the unknown — both to learner and faculty and to science itself. Secondly it must be a question that can be worked upon and that work has the potential to contribute both to the individual and to knowledge. In a sense, all good questions are essentially the same — how does one see what one has never seen before, even though one may have looked a thousand times? The distinctions between faculty and trainee blur when addressing such a question. Both become investigators. Each has the potential to help the other move further and understand more than either could have accomplished alone. Good questions are not always easily formulated, and the interactional process between instructor and learner can be a delicate balance. A great deal depends upon the abilities of the instructor.

The clinician is continually tempted to fit observations of a family to a preconceived set of notions about the nature of family behavior. Yet the effort to fit the facts to one's own view is the heart of subjectivity and obscures an accurate, broader viewpoint. In a similar fashion, the learner is tempted to build a way of thinking about a family on a single observation or insight. The mind makes connections and interpretations that have no factual basis. The resulting vision of a family rests more on imagination than on fact.

In the training as in the clinical setting, the process moves from observation to reflection and back to observation, where imagination can be compared to what is factual. There are, of course, any number of difficult questions in such a process. The teacher is as vulnerable as the learner to the construction of an imagined reality. He or she must be aware of the difference between speculation and fact. This implies an awareness of the limits of one's own knowledge. Sometimes the learner is more objective than the instructor and may see flaws in the mentor's imagined reality. At such times the teacher has more to learn from his pupil than the other way around. Care must be taken that a learner's careful reflection is not labeled resistance. Such labeling is akin to processes in a family that define a particular individual as the problem. At that point, a systems perspective is lost.

The nature of observation and the relationship between observation and thought or reflection are areas of interest. While human perception is probably always subjective to some degree, one can strive for increased objectivity. An important and basic question for teacher and learner alike concerns objectivity. How does one observe a family objectively? What is the difference between a subjective and an objective observation? How does one work toward becoming a more objective observer of the world.

In many ways training in Family Systems Theory is about the process of thinking. How a one thinks — rather than what one thinks — assumes basic importance. Systems thinking is based in a broad perspective rather than a narrow one. It also involves recognizing and challenging firmly held assumptions about human nature and behavior. It places a high premium on identifying facts of human behavior, particularly as they occur within the family network. The effort to expand perspective, challenge assumptions, and note facts becomes central to the effort to see the world differently, to apprehend that which one has never recognized before.

The focus on objectivity goes hand-in-hand with questions about thinking. Trainer and trainee alike grapple with what is factual about a family. What is the difference between a fact, an opinion, a belief, and a conviction? What is the difference between a family and a group or a family and an organization? Is there any? How does one know? Is the evidence factual or does it represent someone's opinion? These questions, and dozens of others like them, lie at the heart of training in Bowen Family Systems Theory.

Even simple questions like what is factual about a family require careful consideration. Vital statistics, such as births, deaths, changes in location, and changes in health, are generally verifiable. A different level of thinking and observation is required when one attempts to make factual statements about a family as a unit. What happens, how, when, where it happens, and who is involved can be observed and generally verified. With such information it is possible to make factual statements about difficult concepts or abstractions. What people say is generally less important than what they do or how they react when they are talking about a difficult idea or subject. The feelings and thoughts are not observable. Their effects, expressed in relationship, are. Discrepancies between how one thinks about a family and what one observes are important to note. Each such deviation from what one expects has the potential to expand one's understanding of a particular family and of families in general. It is often more efficient to look for what does not fit one's notions than to look for evidence to support them.

People do not find it easy to think about familiar things in new ways. The process of apprehending something differently seems to require many efforts with a mixture of failures and partial successes. The task is lengthy, although with diligent effort most seem able to broaden perspective, loosen conditioned ways of thinking and understanding, and "see" in ways never before possible.

Consequently training in Bowen Family Systems Theory is considered a long-term process, not easily measured in terms of time spent in a particular training program. Time spent in a training program does not necessarily produce learning and competency. People learn differently. A beginner intuitively and naturally may think with greater breadth and clarity than an advanced student with several years training. Some understand an idea or concept at first meeting, and others never grasp it no matter how long they try. The situation is further complicated by different levels of understanding. One can have some understanding of ideas without seeing how they apply to the world or to oneself. For this reason the Family Center has avoided offering short-term training. Each training segment lasts one year, and several segments are believed necessary for an adequate beginning. Many who participate in a program continue their contact with the Family Center for several years beyond the completion of their initial training.

All training programs include didactic and supervisory components. In the didactic sessions a faculty member presents his or her current thinking about a particular area of interest or theory. The presentation may be specifically directed to Bowen Theory or may range more broadly to other areas of interest. Occasionally the session will focus on the clinical work of the faculty member. Such relatively formal presentations may include lectures, instructional videotapes, and panel discussions. Each presentation is followed by a period for questions and discussion.

The Family Center maintains a large library of videotapes of clinical sessions with families. New tapes are added monthly as faculty members take turns interviewing families for a clinical conference series. The videotape series now spans almost twenty-five years. In addition tapes are made for teaching purposes. Generally these tapes present points of theoretical interest and are not recordings of clinical sessions. While such instructional tapes are used in training, only rarely are tapes of clinical sessions shown. There seems to be a tendency for viewers to lose sight of theory and focus intently on techniques when watching these tapes. Such a focus works against the direction of training at the Family Center. Consequently the library of faculty tapes remains an archive for future research only.

Supervisory sessions involve a small number of people (three to six) meeting with a faculty member. Participants present current clinical work, report on their thinking about and efforts with their own families, and raise questions of interest to them. With beginning trainees, the faculty member may spend part of the time illustrating and clarifying basic concepts. Participants may present videotapes or audiotapes of their own clinical work.

A simple principle operates in the conduct of many supervisory and didactic sessions in the training program. The presenter or supervisor attempts to define his or her thinking as clearly as possible and to engage the thinking, reflective capacity of the other. The effort is to define self and broaden thinking, not to change the beliefs or thinking of the other. The point is simply to keep the interaction between instructor and learner as thoughtful as possible, to respect the differences in the way people think about the world and at the same time to expand perspective where possible. This is essentially similar to the goal of the clinician with the family.

The effort and progress of a learner can be evaluated using the general framework used to describe the activity of the coach. How well does the learner display (1) the effort to become a more accurate observer of self and the family; (2) the development of personal relationships with each member of the family; (3) the effort to increase one's ability to control emotional reactivity to the family; and (4) the sustained effort to remain neutral or detriangled while relating to the emotional issues of the family?

Much more is involved than simply the frequency of visits made to the family and what is said during the visit. How well does the trainee understand his or her own role in the family processes? What sort of efforts has the individual undertaken to increase understanding? Does the learner have an awareness of and respect for the strength of emotional processes in the family? Is his or her focus more on self in the family or on trying to fix the family's "problem"?

Another area for evaluation concerns the quality of thinking the learner displays. This is a difficult and elusive area. To "think systems" is not an easy task. How well can the learner see a big picture and not become enmeshed in details? Does the trainee have an appreciation of complexity, or is he or she caught up in simplistic answers to difficult problems? Does the individual have a way of monitoring his or her own subjectivity? To what extent can the person entertain ideas for their own merit without automatically trying to fit them into an existing viewpoint? Does the trainee appreciate the long-term nature of the effort toward differentiation of self?

A milestone is reached when the learner becomes an investigator, substituting the active pursuit of knowledge for the passive receipt and reproduction of information. At that point the student begins to contribute to the effort to press ahead into new or poorly understood territory. The distinction between instructor and learner blurs as the interaction between them spurs each to stretch further than either could alone. This sort of dynamism is not easily attained nor maintained. But, in a sense, the training programs in Bowen Theory, if they are successful, aim toward the establishment of this process.

Successful trainees at some point begin to contribute to the development of family theory and the understanding of human behavior. Any well thought out theory presents countless questions about the nature of the phenomenon it attempts to describe. These questions, and others as yet unrecognized, form the outline for future study and theoretical development. Bowen Theory is no exception. Many broad avenues exist for further investigation and study.

Facts about nature come from many and varied sources. The work of all natural scientists is of great interest, and not only that work which is directly concerned with human behavior or the human family. Theory is dynamic, always shifting slightly in response to new facts and observation. Where fact and thinking disagree, theory must change. Nature takes precedence over thought and is never wrong.

A theory of natural systems does not exclude any facet of knowledge of the natural world, from the realm of the smallest microorganism to the immense ocean ranges of the whale. There is as yet no broad theory of natural systems. Bowen Theory is limited to the natural system of the human family. Yet work in other areas of science appears to move toward such a broad theory. At some point in the future, it may be possible to link theory about the natural system of the family to a broader natural systems theory. In some fashion or another, almost all work at the Family Center aims toward a possible contribution to such a theory of natural systems.

A new theory also highlights many new areas of potential application. Each of these areas can be defined and investigated. The notion of the family as a unit is clearly a systems concept and appears to have implications for the understanding and treatment of various disease processes. The family's emotional climate or state may play a role in the emergence of clinical symptoms in a particular individual. To the extent that this is so, people other than the patient can influence the progress of the illness by their own efforts within the unit. To the extent that functional differentiation can be enhanced, patients and families can manage the course of illness with greater maturity and dignity than otherwise possible. While the concept is clear and anecdotal and clinical evidence tends to support theory, much remains to be thought through and investigated in this arena.

The broad phenomenon generally referred to as *emotional reactivity* must play a role in such considerations of the family unit and illness. The sensitivity of the organism can be monitored, at least in a simple manner. Many trainees become involved in studies of physiology, using biofeedback mechanisms to enhance their efforts. How does interpersonal interaction affect the physiological parameters being measured? How do such effects correlate with disease processes? Such complex questions are challenging but have the potential to expand greatly the understanding of human functioning.

The concept of differentiation itself is far from fully explored and clarified. What is the interplay of heredity, the internal states of the organism, and the environment which produces the levels of functional and basic differentiation? Is differentiation applicable beyond the realm of the human? Does it exist in other animals? If so, how can it be recognized and how does it function in those species that display it? Each of the other concepts of Bowen Theory pose similar intriguing questions for further investigation.

Emotional forces in society are another manifestation of emotional reactivity. Processes in society, therefore, are another area of attention. To what extent does human emotionality play a role in social dilemmas? How is conflict to be understood? What sorts of mechanisms underlie the various crises and fads of social living? To what degree is the human capable of avoiding the emotional traps or behavioral sinks outlined by Calhoun (Chapter 1) in his work with small mammals? Crisis and dilemma appear unavoidable for humankind in the coming century. Family Systems Theory and/or a theory of natural systems may provide some insight and direction to coming generations in their effort to live in harmony with one another and with other living things on the planet.

Bowen Family Systems Theory is a product of the effort to move toward a new frontier. Training within the framework of Bowen Theory attempts to be as consistent as possible with the directions suggested by the theory itself. At the same time, a counter-balancing effort is required to offset the tendency to turn theory into dogma, thus blinding a "follower" to a world beyond the limits of his or her narrow vision. At its best, such training allows the individual to press ahead into the unknown, guided by theory and thought, toward the promise of new science, a science of the human.

Index

Adaptation, 12–13, 15, 58
Adaptivity of spouses, 56–58
Aggression, 12
Animal studies, 5–14
Anxiety, 31, 44, 75, 83
  definitions of, 42, 67
  expression to children, 55–59
  emotional distance and, 52–55,
    88–89
  marital conflict and, 53–54, 56–58
  role in family functioning, 38–39
  social climate and, 64–65
  togetherness and, 43
  within triangles, 49–51
Appearance, 32
Attachment, 29–31
  management of, 62–63
  between mother and child, 37–38
  predator-prey, 16–17
Autonomy, 43
Awareness, levels of, 38

B family, 83–98
Behavior patterns, 1–2, 7–9, 24, 46
Behavioral sink, 14
Beliefs, 48
Bertalanffy, Ludwig von, 3
Biochemistry of cells, 24
Biosphere, 21–22
Birth order. See Sibling position
Bonding, 30, 33, 36
Bowen, Murray, 1–3
Bowen Family Systems Theory,
  37–66, 100–101, 104–109
Brain, 6-8
Breeding pair, 28–29, 30–35

Calhoun, John B., 5, 9–15, 97
Case study of B family, 83–98
Cells, 23–25
Central nervous system, 25
Children, 32–33

invested, 60
  parental response to, 58–59
  responsibility for self, 32
  transmission of problem to, 54–56
Clinical analysis, 87–90
Clinical practice, family systems
  theory in, 67–82
Clinician, role of in case
  study, 83–84
Closeness-distance cycle, 38–39
Coaching, 77–78
Colonies, 25–26
Conceptual space, 14
Crowding, 14, 64
Cycles, closeness-distance, 38–39

Darwin, Charles, 2, 27
Deceptive behavior, 7
Depression, 62, 84
Detriangle process of therapist, 73–
  75. See also neutrality of
  clinician
Diagram, family, 68–70, 86
Differentiation, 15, 34–35, 44, 83
  by children, 60
  concept of, 47
  marital partners and, 51–52, 60
  level in society, 64
  of self, 35, 45–48, 67–68, 90, 101–103
  of therapist, 89–92
  scale of, 40
DNA, 24
Doves, 29–30

Emotion, 5, 7–8, 27, 40–42, 45, 101
  awareness of, 38
  between spouses, 72–73
  cutoff, 45, 62–63
  distance, 52–53
  family processes, 88–90
  functioning of, 88-90
  illness, 4–5, 16